KU-559-573

A SOCIALIST AND WAR

A SOCIALIST AND WAR

1914-1916

by

JAMES CONNOLLY

Edited and with an Introduction by

P. J. MUSGROVE

LONDON
LAWRENCE & WISHART LTD

First published 1941

Printed in Great Britain by
Billing and Sons Ltd., Guildford and Esher

"In the long run the freedom of a nation is measured by the freedom of its lowest class; every upward step of that class to the possibility of possessing higher things raises the standard of the nation in the scale of civilization; every time that class is beaten back into the mire, the whole moral tone of the nation suffers. Condemned and despised though he be, yet the rebellious docker is the sign and symbol to all that an imperfect civilization cannot last, for slavery cannot survive the awakened intelligence of the slave."

JAMES CONNOLLY.

(From an editorial in the first issue of Connolly's paper, *The Workers' Republic*, May 29th, 1915.)

CONTENTS

INTRODUCTION

JAMES CONNOLLY'S execution in 1916 not only robbed Ireland of a sturdy fighter for Trade Unionism and Irish independence, but deprived the international socialist movement of one of its most advanced leaders. Born near Clones, Co. Monaghan, in 1870, his father was a labourer, and from his earliest years James Connolly waged a struggle with poverty. When he was ten years old his family were forced, like so many others of their class, to seek work in Scotland, and here Connolly received his early experience of the socialist movement and joined the Social Democratic Federation. From this time to the day he was carried wounded on a stretcher (some say already dying) to face a British firing squad, Jim Connolly never wavered in his struggles on behalf of the working class of the world.

In Britain, Ireland and America (where for a time he was a member of the Socialist Labour Party and Organizer for the Industrial Workers of the World) Connolly's sincerity and ability as a leader gained him the respect of the organized workers. When he returned to Ireland from America in 1910 he was appointed Organizer for the Socialist Party of Ireland and Ulster District Organizer of the Irish Transport Workers' Union. Back in his native Ulster he united Catholics and Protestants, set at each other's throats by the sectarian, splitting policy of the ruling class, in a powerful demand for improvements in their poverty-stricken existence. The dockers on the

Belfast quayside and the hungry mill girls remember to this day Connolly's virile leadership in their industrial battles.

In 1913 Connolly and Jim Larkin led the workers of Dublin in the savage and bloody "labour war" with the organized employers, who made use of all the state machinery in an endeavour to destroy "Larkinism," or in other words the entire Irish Trade Union movement. Through the militancy of the starving Dublin workers and their families, together with the uncompromising leadership of the Irish Transport Workers' Union, the right of organization was preserved. Connolly claimed that it was a "drawn battle."

The 1913 clash of classes in the industrial field saw the birth of Connolly's red army, the Irish Citizen Army, which together with the Irish Volunteers was three years later to strike the first military blow on behalf of Europe's working class against the first Imperialist World War. In the birth and development of the Irish Citizen Army we see a reflection of Connolly's true greatness. He was not merely an uncompromising Trade Union leader, *but he was capable of rising to revolutionary leadership through his acceptance and understanding of basic Marxist principles.* This fundamental basis for Connolly's achievements has been obscured in Ireland, where his clear-cut reasoning has been largely suppressed and distorted. These distortions have served also to bewilder that wider world audience which to-day stands in need of the lessons of his life and leadership.

Connolly's fate in this respect has been the fate of most great revolutionary leaders. Engels was called upon to attack the distortions of Marx's doctrines.

Lenin performed a similar task for both of them, while, more recently, Stalin has been obliged to expose the distortions of Leninism. Lenin concisely states the source and objects of such corruptions.

> "During the lifetime of great revolutionaries, the oppressing classes relentlessly persecute them, treat their teachings with malicious hostility and fierce hatred, and subject them to an unscrupulous campaign of lies and slanders. After their deaths, attempts are made to convert them into harmless icons, to canonize them, so to speak, and to surround their *names* with a certain halo for the 'consolation' of the oppressed classes, and with the object of duping them, while at the same time emasculating the revolutionary doctrine of its content, vulgarizing it and blunting its revolutionary edge. At the present time, the bourgeoisie and the opportunists in the Labour movement concur in this 'revision' of Marxism. They omit, obliterate and distort the revolutionary side of its doctrine, its revolutionary soul. They push to the foreground and extol what is or seems acceptable to the bourgeoisie." [1]

With the exception of a few published works,[2] the writings of James Connolly lie buried in museum files of obscure periodicals. This virtual suppression of the mass of Connolly's writings is but part of the campaign to "omit, obliterate and distort the revolutionary side of its doctrine, its revolutionary soul."

There is yet another, and a most important, aspect of the posthumous evaluation of Connolly. His

[1] *State and Revolution.*

[2] *Labour in Irish History; The Reconquest of Ireland; Labour, Nationality and Religion* and a few smaller pamphlets.

biographer, Desmond Ryan, condemns the "partisan claims on his corpse" (and then hastens to snatch Connolly's body for the now non-socialist Irish Labour Party!). As Arthur McManus pointed out so long ago as 1924,[1] this tendency is, in fact, the most remarkable demonstration of Connolly's place in the heart of the masses. It is most significant that not even the "imperialistic" Labour Party in Northern Ireland or the avowedly Fascist O'Duffy dare openly attack Connolly's memory.

The distortion of Connolly's doctrines, coupled with the undignified scramble of so many puny Irish politicians to bask in the reflected glory of his name (which is invoked, in Eire at least, on the election platform of *every* party), makes it necessary to examine Connolly's actions and teachings in order to establish beyond doubt his true rôle in the Irish and international revolutionary struggle.

Although in this Introduction it is not possible to attempt such a definitive evaluation of Connolly, we may draw important lessons from certain aspects of his activities and teachings which contain valuable lessons for to-day.

The Peasant Movement

A striking example of Connolly's Marxist thought is to be found in his attitude towards the peasant problem, which he studied, not only in its relation to Ireland, but also to England and the Continent.

Until the comparatively recent creation of an Irish proletariat, the driving force of the national struggle

[1] *Communist Review*, May, 1924.

lay with the poor peasantry. Dispossessed of their land, looted by landlordism and, more recently, by finance capital, they rose in spasmodic and localized revolt in every generation for 700 years. This bitter and often starving army, which for many centuries was in effect virtually the entire Irish race, fought for one thing—the land. Local secret organizations carried on an incessant campaign of terrorism against landlords and their agents, occasionally, as in the '70s under the leadership of the Land League, developing on an almost national scale, but always being deceived and betrayed by their middle-class leaders and allies.

The Fenians, however, who, in their struggle for social liberty, joined with the Land League in their struggle for the land, earned Connolly's praise:

> "When the revolutionary Nationalists threw in their lot with the Land League, and made the land struggle the basis for their warfare, they were not only placing themselves in touch once more with those inexhaustible quarries of material interests from whom all the great Irish statesmen from Laurence O'Toole to Wolfe Tone drew the stones upon which they built their edifice of a militant patriotic Irish organization, but they were also, consciously or unconsciously, placing themselves in accord with *the principles which underlie and inspire the modern movement of Labour.*"

Not only was Connolly aware of the importance of peasant support for the revolutionary urban Labour movement, but he clearly saw, long before his theories were tested by the Russian Revolution of 1917, the potential "conflict" between town and country *after the defeat of capitalism.* Like Lenin, he realized the possible rôle of the Co-operatives in securing unity between the proletariat and the peasantry, not only in the economic field, but also eventually in the political field. He writes:[1]

> "If to that combination of agriculturalists and urban labourers we have just hinted at as a possibility of co-operation on the economic field, we add the further possible development of an understanding upon the political field between these two groups of co-operators, we begin to realize the great and fundamental change now slowly maturing in our midst."

Bourgeois Nationalism

Connolly's temporary military alliance with the Irish bourgeois nationalists, which culminated in the 1916 Rising, did not prevent him attacking their leaders continuously in his endeavours to convince the Irish working class and peasantry that "Freedom for Ireland" was a meaningless slogan unless it implied the social freedom of the mass of the Irish people. "We are Republicans *because* we are Socialists," he explained. Emphasizing that he had "no room for illusions about freedom," he consistently hammered home the truth that "the Irish question is a social question. The whole agelong fight of the Irish people against their oppressors resolves itself in the last analysis into a fight for the mastery of the means of life, the sources of production, in Ireland."[2]

Following on this, Connolly declared that the full support of the industrial workers and the peasantry

[1] *Reconquest of Ireland.*
[2] *Labour in Irish History.*

could not be harnessed by bourgeois nationalists who were prepared to fight for political independence, but at the same time turned down the claims to freedom of "the producing classes . . . from social as well as from political bondage." He identified the interests of Ireland with the interests of the working people of Ireland, believing that the true freedom of Ireland could only be attained by the smashing of the connection with the British Empire by the workers and peasants *in order that* they might then proceed to establish socialism.

This fundamental question is one aspect of Connolly's reasoning which has been shelved or obscured. The Northern Ireland Labour Party to-day acknowledges that Connolly was a Socialist, but rejects in practice his policy of struggle against British Imperialism. They prefer to profess "internationalism" as an excuse for tailing behind the British Labour and Trade Union movements. The Labour Party in Eire approves of Connolly's stand in 1916, but is terrified by the "redness" of his social teachings. What both these organizations either fail or refuse to appreciate is the fact that the national struggle for political independence is a step towards the revolutionary working class struggle for socialism.

The Easter Rising

In 1916 many supporters of the British Labour movement were prepared to acknowledge Connolly as a great Socialist theoretician and leader. And then came the Easter Rising. Connolly had long previously struggled for a united revolutionary army, composed not only of his own Citizen Army, but also of the armed forces of the bourgeois nationalists, who possessed a considerable working class and peasant following. About 1,000 men fought the might of the British armed forces for a week, only ceasing fire when the centre of Dublin lay a mass of smoking ruins. Connolly and the other signatories to the Proclamation of the Irish Republic were executed, but their heroism helped to fan resurgent Irish nationalism into the mighty flame which was to damage British Imperialism so greatly in the years to come.

But what was the reaction to that stirring Red Easter of the mass of the British Labour movement? It is true that there were some British workers who saw in the Rising the leadership of a scientific socialist and the militancy of a class-conscious socialist and trade union organization, but it is nevertheless true to say that it was almost universally greeted (and especially by the Labour leaders) with a mystified and forlorn bleating. "Why did he do it? Why did he soil his socialism by joining with those fanatical Irish militarists?" they cried. The I.L.P., for example, was the dominant element in the British Labour movement, and its pacifist and anti-Marxist policy led to its denunciation of Connolly's revolutionary scientific socialism and of the Easter Rising.

Tom Johnston in *Forward* (May 6th, 1916) is a good example of the prevailing attitude:

> "He may, of course, have changed his views. He may have shut his eyes to the lessons of the history he so ably expounded six years ago; the quiet-mannered, soft musical-voiced man who a year ago was lecturing in Hutchinsonstown for the L.R.C. may suddenly have run amok for a bloody revolu-

tion which, apart from its predestination to failure, could not possibly secure, nor lead to the securing, of the Socialist ownership and control which he spent the best part of his life in advocating. He may. But the psychology of it all is a mystery to me."

He continues by saying that he knew "there would be trouble one day in Ireland, somehow or other . . ."[!] but feels that "the mysterious and astounding part of the insensate rebellion last week was the fact that James Connolly was not only implicated in it, but seems to have been one of its organizers."

As Charles Donnelly has pointed out,[1] "Labourism, confronted with revolutionary Socialism, then reached its classic expression, 'The psychology of it all is a mystery to me.' The words seem destined for an epitaph, though not on James Connolly, for whose obituary they were written. . . . The Easter Rising was the culmination of Connolly's method of facing the war, as the Coalition Government was the culmination of the official Labour method of facing it."

As a result of Imperialist propaganda, popular opinion in the British Labour movement inclined to the belief that the Rising was the work of German agents, although the "implication" of Connolly still remained "mysterious and astounding." *Forward* was even more astounded when word came from America that Larkin, Connolly's co-organizer in the Irish Transport Workers' Union, had declared that, not only did he approve of the Rising, but that he had actively assisted in its preparation. Furthermore, he made it clear that Germany neither financed nor con-

[1] *Left Review*, April, 1936.

trolled it. The British Labour movement threw up its hands in despair. Who could ever understand these mad Irish?

The Rising was also condemned as a "putsch." Lenin called it a "heroic rising" and attacked those who made such suggestions.

"Whoever calls such an uprising a 'putsch,'" he declared, "is either a hardened reactionary, or a doctrinaire hopelessly incapable of picturing to himself a social revolution as a living phenomenon."[1] He continues:

> "To imagine that social revolution is *conceivable* without revolts by small nations in the colonies and in Europe, without the revolutionary outbursts of a section of the petty bourgeoisie *with all its prejudices*, without the movement of non-class-conscious proletarian and semi-proletarian masses against the oppression of the landlords, the Church, the Monarchy, the foreign nations, etc.—to imagine that means *repudiating social revolution*. Only those who imagine that in one place an army will line up and say, 'We are for Socialism,' and in another place another army will say, 'We are for imperialism,' and that this will be the social revolution—only those who hold such a ridiculously pedantic opinion could vilify the Irish Rebellion by calling it a 'putsch.'"

He concludes:

> "The misfortune of the Irish is that they rose prematurely, when the European revolt of the proletariat had *not yet* matured. Capitalism is not so harmoniously built that the various springs of rebellion can immediately merge, on their own

[1] *Lenin. Selected Works*, vol. 5, p. 303.

accord, without reverses and defeats. On the other hand, the very fact that revolts break out at different times, in different places, and are of different kinds, guarantees wide scope and depth to the general movement; only in *premature*, partial, sporadic, and therefore unsuccessful, revolutionary movements will the masses gain experience, acquire knowledge, gather strength, get to know their real leaders, the Socialist proletarians, and in this way prepare for the general onslaught, in the same way as separate strikes, demonstrations, local and national, mutinies in the army, outbreaks among the peasantry, etc., prepared the way for the general onslaught in 1905."

This was a true analysis. The 1916 Rising did, in fact, give rise to the mass insurrectionary movement which compelled British Imperialism to make considerable concessions for fear of losing *all* control over Ireland.

The truth is that the 1916 Rising, far from showing any change in Connolly's attitude to the international revolutionary socialist movement, was, in fact, the most striking demonstration that Connolly understood the only manner in which Socialism can be achieved in Ireland. James Connolly's true greatness found its supreme expression in HIS APPRECIATION OF THE RELATION BETWEEN THE NATIONAL REVOLUTIONARY STRUGGLE AND THE REVOLUTIONARY STRUGGLE OF THE WORKING CLASS.

While under sentence of death in Dublin Castle, Connolly is reported[1] to have told his daughter: "The Socialists will never understand why I am here. They will all forget that I am an Irishman." From

[1] *Voice of Labour*, May 10th, 1919.

this isolated statement, Connolly's detractors have attempted to argue that his participation in the Rising was due to his ultimate acceptance of idealistic nationalism instead of to his application of the principles of scientific Socialism. No more malicious distortion of Connolly's outlook could be attempted. We have already seen that the "Socialists" were unable to understand his part in the Rising. They found it "mysterious and astounding." They *did*, in fact, forget that Connolly was an Irishman and that the problems facing the Irish Labour movement were very different to those which occupied *their* minds. The "misconceptions" and "doubts" regarding Connolly's leadership in the insurrection were and are the results of an anti-Marxist policy and its resulting lack of understanding of the tasks confronting working class revolutionary movements *in territories occupied and exploited by Imperialism.*

Although a shrewd observer and critic of working-class struggles in other lands, Connolly, through force of circumstances, was largely deprived of contact with the Bolsheviks and other continental Marxist leaders. Revisionists throughout Europe were then, as always, busily distorting Marxism, while in Britain Marxism was but lightly rooted in the Labour movement. Marxism as developed and applied in Ireland by James Connolly was divorced from the main stream of Marxist development on the Continent. Robbed of guidance and criticism from the leading Marxist thinkers of his time, Connolly was obliged to draw direct from Marx and Engels and develop his thought largely in isolation. His two best-known published works, *Labour in Irish History* and *The Reconquest of*

Ireland, are striking testimony to his genius in doing so.

Under such circumstances, however, it is remarkable not that Connolly committed errors of tactics and theory, but that they were so few. One great error, an error which was later to have disastrous results for the Irish working-class movement, was his failure to create a political party "of a new type," based on democratic centralism and strictly disciplined. (This is not to say that he *denied the necessity* for a strong political organization; he founded the Irish Socialist Republican Party and, in America, the Irish Socialist Federation, where he was also National Organizer for the Socialist Party of America.) Although correctly criticizing the deficiencies of craft unionism, his advocacy of industrial unionism led him to exhibit at times a tendency towards syndicalism and a belief that the struggle in the workshop would *automatically* have its political expression. As a result, after Connolly's execution no experienced Marxist party existed to guide the Irish workers in the trying years that followed. Until the founding of the Communist Party of Ireland, only individual followers in Connolly's tradition remained to carry on the struggle.[1]

Connolly did not live to see the birth of the Communist International, but his name is honoured by those who now carry on the international struggle for world socialism, the ideal for which he worked and for which he gave his life.

Connolly was the complete revolutionary soldier. Starting life with negligible facilities for learning, he mastered several foreign languages, studied Marxist

[1] Among these the name of Liam Mellowes will always be remembered.

economics, literature and the history of the struggles of oppressed classes throughout the world. Connolly's own poetry is widely remembered and quoted, not only in Ireland, but in Britain and America. His versatility is strikingly shown in the production of some of his newspapers. Not only did he write articles, but also he hand-set them, printed them, and completed the process by selling them in the streets.

Connolly's vast store of learning and experience did not lead to dogma, but was a part of his preparation for the struggle. His knowledge of the past was his guide to the future.

As a popular propagandist Connolly can have few equals. A proletarian himself, he was always close to the heart of the people. He knew their hardships because he himself experienced them fully, but, what is more important, he knew also the remedy and succeeded in explaining patiently and simply the only path forward for the workers of the world. The praise and affection of his old comrades in Ireland, Scotland and America testify to his success in presenting the Socialist standpoint from the workers' point of view and in the workers' language.

The articles reprinted in this book demonstrate not only Connolly's qualities as a propagandist and his clear analysis of immediate problems, but also his "internationalism" in the true sense of the word. It is clear from his article herein, "Our Duty in this Crisis," that he viewed the imminent Irish Rising as part of the struggle of the entire European working class. "Starting thus," he says, "Ireland may yet set the torch to a European conflagration that will not burn out until the last throne and the last capitalist bond and debenture will be shrivelled on the funeral pyre of the last warlord."

Connolly's articles in this book make clear his attitude to war. Although revolted by the physical barbarities of warfare, he did not hesitate to lead his Citizen Army into action when the moment came to strike. While "the war of nation against nation in the interest of royal freebooters and cosmopolitan thieves is a thing accursed," he realized that the struggle of exploited nations and classes for freedom is "holy and righteous."

It is impossible to conclude this Introduction without comment on the freshness, and indeed topicality, at the present moment, of these writings which were first published a quarter of a century ago. Connolly revealed and struggled against the impositions of the ruling class during the first Great War as we must do to-day. He recognized the restriction of personal liberty as only another aspect of imperialism's fight for survival. He fought for a free press and for Trade Union rights. He exposed the betrayal of the working class by its leaders' acquiescence, and indeed participation, in repressive legislation and dictatorship. He foresaw and struggled against the lowering of the standard of life of the workers. He realized that the conscription of men who were likely to lose their lives would not be accompanied by the conscription of wealth of those who feared to lose their profits.

These injustices which Connolly exposed are with us to-day in the midst of the second Imperialist World War. It is hoped that the lessons from Connolly's writings may play a part in removing their causes.

Now, as then, the burden of the war rests upon the

working class. Now, as then, the workers must, in Connolly's words, take their stand "nakedly upon their class interests."

I am grateful to the editor of *Forward* for permission to reprint two articles which appeared in that journal. The remaining articles were originally published in two papers, now no longer in existence, *The Irish Worker*, edited by James Larkin, and *The Workers' Republic*, edited by James Connolly himself.

P. J. MUSGROVE.

January, 1941.

A CONTINENTAL REVOLUTION

THE outbreak of war on the Continent of Europe makes it impossible this week to write to *Forward* upon any other question. I have no doubt that to most of my readers Ireland has ere now ceased to be, in colloquial phraseology, the most important place on the map, and that their thoughts are turning gravely to a consideration of the position of the European Socialist movement in the face of this crisis.

Judging by developments up to the time of writing,[1] such considerations must fall far short of affording satisfying reflections to the Socialist thinker. For, what is the position of the Socialist movement in Europe to-day? Summed up briefly it is as follows:

For a generation at least the Socialist movement in all the countries now involved has progressed by leaps and bounds, and more satisfactory still, by steady and continuous increase and development.

The number of votes recorded for Socialist candidates has increased at a phenomenally rapid rate, the number of Socialist representatives in all legislative Chambers has become more and more of a disturbing factor in the calculations of governments; newspapers, magazines, pamphlets and literature of all kinds teaching Socialist ideas have been and are daily distributed by the million amongst the masses; every Army and Navy in Europe has seen a constantly increasing proportion of Socialists

[1] As this article was published on August 16th, 1914, it obviously was written a very few days after the outbreak of war. Connolly's clear analysis of the situation is therefore all the more remarkable.

amongst its soldiers and sailors, and the industrial organizations of the working class have more and more perfected their grasp over the economic machinery of society, and more and more moved responsive to the Socialist conception of their duties. Along with this, hatred of militarism has spread through every rank of society, making everywhere its recruits, and raising an aversion to war even amongst those who in other things accepted the capitalist order of things. Anti-militarist societies and anti-militarist campaigns of Socialist societies and parties, and anti-militarist resolutions of Socialist and International Trade Union Conferences have become part of the order of the day and are no longer phenomena to be wondered at. The whole working class movement stands committed to war upon war—stands so committed at the very height of its strength and influence.

And now, like the proverbial bolt from the blue, war is upon us, and war between the most important, because the most Socialist, nations of the earth. And we are helpless!

What then becomes of all our resolutions, all our protests of fraternization, all our threats of general strikes, all our carefully-built machinery of internationalism, all our hopes for the future? Were they all as sound and fury, signifying nothing? When the German artilleryman, a Socialist serving in the German Army of invasion, sends a shell into the ranks of the French Army, blowing off their heads, tearing out their bowels, and mangling the limbs of dozens of Socialist comrades in that force, will the fact that he, before leaving for the front, "demonstrated" against the war be of any value to the widows and orphans made by the shell he sent upon its mission of murder? Or when the French rifleman pours his murderous rifle fire into the ranks of the German line of attack, will he be able to derive any comfort from the probability that his bullets are murdering or maiming comrades who last year joined in thundering "hochs" and cheers of greeting to the eloquent Jaurès when in Berlin he pleaded for international solidarity? When the Socialist pressed into the Army of the Austrian Kaiser sticks a long, cruel bayonet-knife into the stomach of the Socialist conscript in the Army of the Russian Czar, and gives it a twist so that when pulled out it will pull the entrails out along with it, will the terrible act lose any of its fiendish cruelty by the fact of their common theoretical adhesion to an anti-war propaganda in times of peace? When the Socialist soldier from the Baltic provinces of Russia is sent forward into Prussian Poland to bombard towns and villages until a red trail of blood and fire covers the homes of the unwilling Polish subjects of Prussia, as he gazes upon the corpses of those he has slaughtered and the homes he has destroyed, will he in his turn be comforted by the thought that the Czar whom he serves sent other soldiers a few years ago to carry the same devastation and murder into his own home by the Baltic Sea?

But why go on? Is it not as clear as the fact of life itself that no insurrection of the working class, no general strike, no general uprising of the forces of Labour in Europe could possibly carry with it or entail a greater slaughter of Socialists than will their participation as soldiers in the campaigns of the Armies of their respective countries? Every shell which explodes in the midst of a German battalion will slaughter some Socialists; every Austrian cavalry charge will leave the gashed and hacked bodies of Serbian or Russian Socialists squirming and twisting in agony upon the ground; every Russian, Austrian, or German ship sent to the bottom or blown sky-high will mean sorrow and mourning in the homes of some Socialist comrades of ours. If these men must die, would it not be better to die in their own country fighting for freedom for their class, and for the abolition of war, than to go forth to strange countries and die slaughtering and slaughtered by their brothers that tyrants and profiteers might live?

Civilization is being destroyed before our eyes; the results of generations of propaganda and patient heroic plodding and self-sacrifice are being blown into annihilation from a hundred cannon mouths; thousands of comrades with whose souls we have lived in fraternal communion are about to be done to death; they whose one hope it was to be spared to co-operate in building the perfect society of the future are being driven to fratricidal slaughter in shambles where that hope will be buried under a sea of blood.

I am not writing in captious criticism of my Continental comrades. We know too little about what is happening on the Continent, and events have moved too quickly for any of us to be in a position to criticize at all. But believing as I do that any action would be justified which would put a stop to this colossal crime now being perpetrated, I feel compelled to express the hope that ere long we may read of the paralyzing of the internal transport service on the Continent, even should the act of paralyzing necessitate the erection of Socialist barricades and acts of rioting by Socialist soldiers and sailors, as happened in Russia in 1905. Even an unsuccessful attempt at Social Revolution by force of arms, following the paralysis of the economic life of militarism, would be less disastrous to the Socialist cause than the act of Socialists allowing themselves to be used in the slaughter of their brothers in the cause. A great Continental uprising of the working class would stop the war; a universal protest at public meetings will not save a single life from being wantonly slaughtered.

I make no war upon patriotism; never have done. But against the patriotism of capitalism—the patriotism which makes the interest of the capitalist class the supreme test of duty and right—I place the patriotism of the working class, the patriotism which judges every public act by its effect upon the fortunes of those who toil. That which is good for the working class I esteem patriotic, but that party or movement is the most perfect embodiment of patriotism which most successfully works for the conquest by the working class of the control of the destinies of the land wherein they labour.

To me, therefore, the Socialist of another country is a fellow-patriot, as the capitalist of my own country is a natural enemy. I regard each nation as the possessor of a definite contribution to the common stock of civilization, and I regard the capitalist class of each nation as being the logical and natural enemy of the national culture which constitutes that definite contribution.

Therefore, the stronger I am in my affection for national tradition, literature, language, and sympathies, the more firmly rooted I am in my opposition to that capitalist class which in its soulless lust for power and gold would braze the nations as in a mortar.

Reasoning from such premises, therefore, this war appears to me as the most fearful crime of the centuries. In it the working class are to be sacrificed that a small clique of rulers and armament makers may sate their lust for power and their greed for wealth. Nations are to be obliterated, progress stopped, and international hatreds erected into deities to be worshipped.

(*Forward*, August 15th, 1914.)

OUR DUTY IN THIS CRISIS

WHAT should be the attitude of the working-class democracy of Ireland in face of the present crisis? I wish to emphasize the fact that the question is addressed to the "working-class democracy," because I believe that it would be worse than foolish—it would be a crime against all our hopes and aspirations—to take counsel in this matter from any other source.

Mr. John E. Redmond[1] has just earned the plaudits of all the bitterest enemies of Ireland and slanderers of the Irish race by declaring in the name of Ireland that the British Government can now safely withdraw all its garrisons from Ireland, and that the Irish slaves will guarantee to protect the Irish estate of England until their masters come back to take possession—a statement that announces to all the world that Ireland has at last accepted as permanent this status of a British province. Surely no inspiration can be sought from that source.

The advanced Nationalists have neither a policy nor a leader. During the Russian Revolution[2] such of their Press as existed in and out of Ireland, as well as all their spokesmen, orators and writers, vied with each other in laudation of Russia and vilification of all the Russian enemies of Czardom. It was freely

[1] A leading Irish "Home Ruler" who urged the Irish Volunteers to join the British Army. His nominees were later expelled from the Volunteers' Provisional Committee.

[2] The reference is, of course, to the 1905 Revolution.

asserted that Russia was the natural enemy of England, that the heroic revolutionists were in the pay of the English Government, and that every true Irish patriot ought to pray for the success of the armies of the Czar. Now, as I, amongst other Irish Socialists, predicted all along, when the exigencies of diplomacy make it suitable, the Russian bear and the English lion are hunting together, and every victory for the Czar's Cossacks is a victory for the paymasters of those Scottish Borderers who, but the other day, murdered the people of Dublin in cold blood. Surely the childish intellects that conceived of the pro-Russian campaign of nine years ago cannot give us light and leading in any campaign for freedom from the British allies of Russia to-day? It is well to remember also that in this connection since 1909 the enthusiasm for the Russians was replaced in the same quarter by as blatant a propaganda in favour of the German War Lord. But, since the guns did begin to speak in reality, this propaganda has died out in whispers, whilst without a protest the manhood of Ireland was pledged to armed warfare against the very power our advanced Nationalist friends have wasted so much good ink in acclaiming.

Of late, sections of the advanced Nationalist Press have lent themselves to a desperate effort to misrepresent the position of the Carsonites,[1] and to claim for them the admiration of Irish Nationalists on the grounds that these Carsonites were fearless Irishmen who had refused to take dictation from England. A more devilishly mischievous and lying doctrine was

[1] The Orange followers of Sir Edward Carson and James Craig (the late Lord Craigavon).

never preached in Ireland. The Carsonite position is indeed plain—so plain that nothing but sheer perversity of purpose can misunderstand it, or cloak it with a resemblance to Irish patriotism. The Carsonites say that their fathers were planted in this country to assist in keeping the natives down in subjection that this country might be held for England; that this was God's will because the Catholic Irish were not fit for the responsibilities and powers of free men, and that they are not fit for the exercise of these responsibilities and powers till this day. "Therefore," say the Carsonites, "we have kept our side of the bargain; we have refused to admit the Catholics to power and responsibility; we have maimed the government of this country for England, we propose to continue to do so, and rather than admit that these Catholics—these 'mickies and teagues'—are our equals, we will fight, in the hope that our fighting will cause the English people to revolt against their Government and re-establish us in our historic position as an English colony in Ireland, superior to, and unhampered by, the political institutions of the Irish natives."

How this can be represented as the case of Irishmen refusing to take dictation from England passes all comprehension. It is rather the case of a community in Poland after 250 years' colonization still refusing to adopt the title of natives, and obstinately clinging to the position and privileges of a dominant colony. Their programme is summed up in the expression which forms the dominant note of all their speeches, sermons, and literature—

> "We are loyal British subjects. We hold this country for England. England cannot desert us."

What light or leading, then, can Ireland get from the hysterical patriots who so egregiously misrepresent this fierce contempt for Ireland as something that ought to win the esteem of Irishmen?

What ought to be the attitude of the working class democracy of Ireland in face of the present crisis?

In the first place, then, we ought to clear our minds of all the political cant which would tell us that we have either "natural enemies" or "natural allies" in any of the powers now warring. When it is said that we ought to unite to protect our shores against the "foreign enemy," I confess to be unable to follow that line of reasoning, as I know of no foreign enemy of this country except the British Government, and know that it is not the British Government that is meant.

In the second place we ought to seriously consider that the evil effects of this war upon Ireland will be simply incalculable, that it will cause untold suffering and misery amongst the people, and that as this misery and suffering has been brought upon us because of our enforced partisanship with a nation whose Government never consulted us in the matter, we are therefore perfectly at liberty morally to make any bargain we may see fit, or that may present itself in the course of events. . . .

Should the working class of Europe, rather than slaughter each other for the benefit of kings and financiers, proceed to-morrow to erect barricades all over Europe, to break up bridges and destroy the transport service that war might be abolished, we should be perfectly justified in following such a glorious example and contributing our aid to the final dethronement of the vulture classes that rule and rob the world.

But pending either of these consummations it is our manifest duty to take all possible action to save the poor from the horrors this war has in store.

Let it be remembered that there is no natural scarcity of food in Ireland. Ireland is an agricultural country, and can normally feed all her people under any sane system of things. But prices are going up in England, and hence there will be an immense demand for Irish produce. To meet that demand all nerves will be strained on this side, the food that ought to feed the people of Ireland will be sent out of Ireland in greater quantities than ever, and FAMINE PRICES WILL COME IN IRELAND TO BE IMMEDIATELY FOLLOWED BY FAMINE ITSELF. Ireland will starve, or rather the townspeople of Ireland will starve, that the British army and navy and jingoes may be fed. Remember, the Irish farmer like all other farmers will benefit by the high prices of the war, but these high prices will mean starvation to the labourers in the towns. But without these labourers the farmers' produce cannot leave Ireland without the help of a garrison that England cannot now spare. We must consider at once whether it will not be our duty to refuse to allow agricultural produce to leave Ireland until provision is made for the Irish working class.

Let us not shrink from the consequences. This may mean more than a transport strike, it may mean armed battling in the streets to keep in this country the food for our people. But whatever it may mean it must not be shrunk from. It is the immediately feasible policy of the Working Class Democracy, the answer to all the weaklings who in this crisis of our country's history stand helpless and bewildered, crying for guidance, when they are not hastening to betray her.

Starting thus, Ireland may yet set the torch to a European conflagration that will not burn out until the last throne and the last capitalist bond and debenture will be shrivelled on the funeral pyre of the last war lord.

(*Irish Worker*, August 8th, 1914.)

A MARTYR FOR CONSCIENCE SAKE

AS I am writing this the news appears in the Press that our Comrade, Dr. Karl Liebknecht, has been shot in Germany for refusing to accept military service in the war. The news is unconfirmed, and will, I trust be found later to be untrue,[1] but I propose to take it this week as a text for my article.

Supposing, then, that it were true, what would be the Socialist attitude toward the martyrdom of our beloved Comrade? There can be little hesitation in avowing that all Socialists would endorse his act, and look upon his death as a martyrdom for our cause. And yet if his attitude were correct, what can be said of the attitude of all those Socialists who have gone to the front, and still more of all those Socialists who from Press and platform are urging that nothing should be done now that might disturb the harmony that ought to exist at home, or spoil the wonderful solidarity of the nation in this great crisis?

As far as I can understand these latter, their argument seems to be that they did their whole duty when they protested against the war, but that now that war has been declared it is right that they also should arm in defence of their common country, and act in all things along with their fellow-subjects—those same fellow-subjects whose senseless clamour brought on this awful outburst of murder. We are told, for instance, that the same policy is being pursued by all Socialist

[1] The rumour was, of course, unfounded. On January 15, 1919, however, Karl Liebknecht and Rosa Luxembourg were brutally murdered by German officers, following their arrest by the Social Democratic Government.

parties; that the French Socialists protested against the war—and then went to the front, headed by Gustave Hervé, the great anti-militarist: the German Socialists protested against the war—and then, in the Reichstag, unanimously voted 250 millions to carry it on; the Austrians issued a manifesto against the war—and are now on the frontier doing great deeds of heroism against the foreign enemy; and the Russians erected barricades in the streets of St. Petersburg against the Cossacks, but immediately war was declared went off to the front arm in arm with their Cossack brothers.[1] And so on. Now, if all this is true, what does it mean? It means that the Socialist parties of the various countries mutually cancel each other, and that as a consequence Socialism ceases to exist as a world force, and drops out of history in the greatest crisis of the history of the world, in the very moment when courageous action will most influence history.

We know that not more than a score of men in the various Cabinets of the world have brought about this war, that no European people was consulted upon the question, that preparations for it have been going on for years, and that all the alleged "reasons" for it are so many afterthoughts invented to hide from us the fact that the intrigues and schemes of our rulers had brought the world to this pass. All Socialists are agreed upon this. Being so agreed, are we now to forget it all: to forget all our ideas of human brotherhood, and because some twenty highly-placed criminals say our country requires us to slaughter our brothers beyond

[1] It was, of course, impossible for Connolly to have learned by the time of writing of the stand which was being taken by the Russian Bolsheviks. Some time later news of this reached him.

the seas or the frontiers, are we bound to accept their statement, and proceed to *slaughter our comrades abroad at the dictate of our enemies at home*? The idea outrages my every sense of justice and fraternity. I may be only a voice crying in the wilderness, a crank amongst a community of the wise; but whoever I be, I must, in deference to my own self-respect, and to the sanctity of my own soul, protest against the doctrine that any decree of theirs of national honour can excuse a Socialist who serves in a war which he has denounced as a needless war, can absolve from the guilt of murder any Socialist who at the dictate of a Capitalist Government draws the trigger of a rifle upon or sends a shot from a gun into the breasts of people with whom he has no quarrel, and who are his fellow-labourers in the useful work of civilization.

We have for years informed the world that we were in revolt against the iniquities of modern civilization, but now we hear Socialists informing us that it is our duty to become accomplices of the rulers of modern civilization in the greatest of all iniquities, the slaughter of man by his fellow man; and that as long as we make our formal protest we have done our whole duty and can cheerfully proceed to take life, burn peaceful homes, and lay waste fields smiling with food!

Our Comrade, Dr. Liebknecht, if he has died rather than admit this new doctrine, has died the happiest death that man can die, has put to eternal shame the thousands of "Comrades" in every European land who, with the cant of brotherhood upon their lips, have gone forth in the armies of the Capitalist rulers—murdering and to murder. The old veteran leader of German

Social Democracy, his father, Wilhelm Liebknecht, said in one of his small pamphlets that—

> "*The working class of the world has but one enemy—the capitalist class of the world, those of their own country at the head of the list.*"[1]

Well and truly has the son lived up to the truly revolutionary doctrine of the father: lived and died for its eternal truth and wisdom.

Now we are hearing a new excuse for the complicity of Socialists in this war. It is that this war will be the last war, its horrors will be so great that humanity will refuse to allow another.

The homely Irish proverb has it that "far off cows have long horns," or that "far away hills are always green." It must have been in some such spirit that this latest argument was evolved. For what can happen in the future that is not more applicable now? In the future this militarist spirit will probably be in the ascendant, new national prejudices will have been born, new international hatreds called forth. There will be memories of recent defeats to wipe out, fresh frontiers to conserve or to obliterate, and the military caste will have acquired an ascendency over the popular imagination because the large numbers of the various armies will have given rise to widespread solicitude for their welfare and consequent hopes for their success. If you have friends or relatives whom you dearly love serving in the army, you cannot help wishing for the success of that army and the defeat

[1] Karl Liebknecht himself writes: "The proletariat knows that the fatherland, for which it must fight, is not its fatherland, that in every country it has only one real foe—the capitalist class which oppresses and exploits it." (*Militarism and Anti-Militarism.*)

of its immediate opponents, and from such a state of feeling to the most intense Jingoism is but a small and easy transition. The large armies of to-day draw upon the whole population; all are interested in the fate of their friends or relatives, and we may all be sure that the lying Press can be depended upon to convert solicitude for our friends into passionate hatred for those whom war makes their opponents.

No; we cannot draw upon the future for a draft to pay our present duties. There is no moratorium to postpone the payment of the debt the Socialists owe to the cause; it can only be paid now. Paid it may be in martyrdom, but a few hundred such martyrdoms would be but a small price to pay to avert the slaughter of hundreds of thousands. If our German Comrade, Liebknecht, has paid the price, perhaps the others may yet nerve themselves for that sacrifice. On what conception of national honour can we blame them? Before what fetish of national dignity can we prostrate ourselves in abasement to atone for their act?

The war of a subject nation for independence, for the right to live out its own life in its own way, may and can be justified as holy and righteous; the war of a subject class to free itself from the debasing conditions of economic and political slavery should at all times choose its own weapons, and hold and esteem all as sacred instruments of righteousness, but the war of nation against nation in the interest of royal freebooters and cosmopolitan thieves is a thing accursed.

All hail, then, to our continental Comrade, who, in a world of imperial and financial brigands and cowardly trimmers and compromisers, showed mankind that men still know how to die for the holiest of all causes—the sanctity of the human soul, the practical brotherhood of the human race!

(*Forward*, August 22nd, 1914.)

AMERICA AND EUROPE

CERTAIN English Press agencies and their Irish imitators have during the past fortnight been hard at work assuring the reading public that in the United States public opinion is practically unanimous on the side of Great Britain and her allies.[1] It would be as well for the readers of the *Irish Worker* to take that statement with the proverbial grain of salt and bucket of sea-water. It is as true probably as the currently accepted English yarn that the United States is a great Anglo-Saxon nation—a yarn that is blatantly asserted by all English politicians and journalists and greedily swallowed by most working people in England despite the fact that ten minutes' calm reflection upon the history of immigration into America would show that the Anglo-Saxon in that country represents but a very small drop in a very big ocean of races. Somewhat similar reflection upon facts will serve to dispel the idea of the solid American sentiment for England. The present writer does not know from personal knowledge the present state of public opinion in the States, but he does know from personal knowledge the various elements of which the population of the

[1] This propaganda of 1914 is significant when we consider the present press campaign boosting the "moral support" and "identity of interests" between Britain and the U.S.A. *The Star*, October 10th, 1940, declared in headlines that "U.S. Has One Foot in the War." The voices of the millions of U.S. citizens who are crying for peace are not allowed to reach us through the capitalist Press. The *Daily Worker* (October 11th, 1940) was the only paper to publish in full the appeal of Earl Browder, Communist Presidential Candidate, for a peace policy based upon friendship with China and the U.S.S.R.

States is composed, and he knows their usual affiliation and political leanings. And from such knowledge it is not hard to guess at the state of public sentiment upon this war.

Next to the native-born Americans, who although derived from all races are in all things loyal first to American interests and American ideas, the two greatest elements in America are the Irish and the Germans. Of the German-American population, then, it may be quite safe to say that their sentiments are most likely with the Fatherland, even although they may be entirely opposed to the German Government. The German Press is the most powerful Press in America not printed in the English language. It is read not only by all German immigrants and their children, but as the German language is a sort of *lingua franca* or free common language to Hungarians, Poles, Lithuanians, Czechs, Slavs and Jews, it is read by all those races and nationalities likewise. One may be sure that the German journalists have kept well to the front the fact that the German Government offered to concede all that the British Government had asked for in the matter of Belgium, and had even asked the British Government to name its own terms of neutrality, and that the British Foreign Minister concealed this fact from the Parliament when speaking before the declaration of war. One may be sure that such a typical act of British double-dealing has not been allowed to escape the attention of the readers of the German-American Press. Nor yet is it likely that the non-German elements of the foreign-speaking population in America are any more in favour of the Allies than the Germans. Belgians and French are numerically insignificant in that country in proportion to the North and South Europeans.

The Hungarians are not likely either from present national reasons, from Socialistic sympathies, or from their past traditions to favour any policy likely to increase the favour of their Russian neighbours in Europe—the Russians whose armies in 1848 laid Hungary in ruins in order to drive the Hungarian revolutionists back under the heel of Austria; the Russians whose brutal despotism is the perpetual menace of every freedom-aspiring community from the Black Sea to the Baltic. The Finns, most enlightened and most progressive of all the races within or bordering upon that vast stretch of territory, may well be trusted to work and pray for the humiliation of the Russian tyrant whose hand is even now upon their throat, whose Cossacks were but yesterday trampling into the dust their laws, their language, their liberties, their very existence as a separate people, and so trampling despite all treaties to the contrary. The people of the Baltic provinces were but the other day harried with fire and sword by the Russian allies of the British Lion. They have swarmed into America to escape the fury; can they be wishing for the success of the allies of Russia? Not the most numerically important, but surely one of the most influential of the races represented in America are the Jews. Particularly is this true of the eastern states, and in the commercial and journalistic world. I observe that in one of the recent proclamations the Russian Czar speaks of his "beloved Jews" in calling them to the army. English newspapers speak with tender admiration of such Imperial manifestos; honest workers can only feel sickened by the thought of this imperial bully whose passion it is to torture, imprison and slaughter in times of peace those to whom he appeals with snivelling panic in times of war.

Conscientious and impartial authorities have proven from official documents that the pogroms or race riots for which Russia has been notorious, and of which the Jews are the victims, have almost always been the work of Government agents, and have always been carried out with Government connivance. In these pogroms the Jewish districts were given up to pillage and outrage by mobs of armed men, whilst the police looked calmly on. Shops and houses were burned after being looted, women and children were ravished, babies and old men and women were thrown from windows to their death in the streets, and hell was let loose generally upon the defenceless people. After long months some few nobodies were occasionally arrested and sentenced for these crimes, only to be set free again by pardon *signed by the Czar's own hand*. And now this same Czar addressing the unfortunate survivors calls them his "beloved Jews."

Verily there must be laughter in hell these days.

Surely the Jews are not unanimously wishing for the success of the British armies which are fighting to increase the power of this monster over Europe.

And the Poles; is it possible that they, like the fool Irish, will rush out to fight for their tyrant, for the tyrant whose prisons are full of their compatriots? Or that the Poles in America are praying for the success of the Russian Czar?

Certainly the Press tells us with tears of joy dropping from their printing machines that the manifesto to the Poles promises complete autonomy to Poland, and that in view of that promise the Poles will be radiantly joyous with enthusiasm for the Czar. Ah, promises! How easily promises fall from the lips of tyrants! Remember the words of Whitman, the "good grey poet" of America, when writing on the promises of European Royalty to the revolutionists of 1848.

> "For many a promise made by Royal lips, and broken,
> And laughed at in the breaking."

The Poles know, the Revolutionists of the world know, if others have forgotten, that in his manifesto of October, 1905, this same Czar guaranteed in his own words that the population of all Russia and Poland was to be

> "given the inviolable foundation of civil rights, based on the actual inviolability of the person, and freedom of belief, of speech, of organization, and meeting,"

and that as soon as his Government had crushed the revolution "those who tried to realize these principles were treated as rebels guilty of high treason," as Prince Kropotkin truly remarks.

One small item will illustrate the fidelity of the Czar to his own royal promises. For trying to act up to the principles laid down by the Czar as above there were exiled to Siberia by administrative order—that is to say without trial—in 1908 no less a number of political prisoners than 74,000. These are the figures as supplied by the Department of Police to the Russian Duma upon the request of that body for exact information.

We are scarcely likely to hear of the subjects of the Czar who have escaped to America swelling the chorus of prayers for the success of Russia and her ally, Great Britain.

Next to the Germans the largest and most respected non-English speaking element in the States are the Scandinavians, Danes, Norwegians and Swedes. The largest in numbers are the Swedes, who indeed rather dominate the others. The attitude of the Swedes towards the war and their prayers for the victor can easily be judged if we remember the question that formed the issue upon which the last general election in Sweden was fought. That issue was the Government demand for more soldiers, more ships, and more fortresses to protect Sweden against Russia.

It was freely declared that the anxiety of the Russian Czar to wrest her liberties from Finland and to Russianize her armies was a mere preliminary to open the way for a conquest of Sweden. Hence Sweden and all the Scandinavian countries and all their friends abroad feel that the present campaign of the Triple Alliance, France, England and Russia, is a campaign to make the Russian despot the overlord and master of all the free countries of Northern Europe, as the struggling peoples of Southern Europe feel that the same campaign is designed to place the greatest enemies of social and political freedom in an impregnable position of military strength.

It is felt, in short, that England is sacrificing the hopes of civilization in Europe in order to safeguard her commercial prestige and destroy a successful commercial rival; just as it is felt that the capitalist class in France in lending money to the Russian Czar during the Revolution of 1905 struck down the hopes of Freedom in Russia, and in order to secure the dividends upon that unholy loan are now needlessly plunging their country into war—betraying a republic in order to support an autocracy to which they have lent money.

These are the considerations of which the Irish Press is for the most part laughably ignorant, and of which they suppress all mention when they do know, but which are perfectly well known to the American public.

Do not let us therefore worry over the carefully manufactured lies of the news agencies as to the attitude of the great American public. For the native-born Americans, suffice to say that to aid their judgment they have a rooted inherited distrust of England, and a dislike of Russia born of broad human sympathies and love of liberty.

Finally, as a word of warning this week. Do not let anyone play upon your sympathies by denunciation of the German military bullies. German military bullies, like all tyrannies among civilized people, need fear nothing so much as native (German) democracy. Attacks from outside only strengthen tyrants within a nation. If we had to choose between strengthening the German bully or the Russian autocrat the wise choice would be on the side of the German. For the German people are a highly civilized people, responsive to every progressive influence, and rapidly forging weapons for their own emancipation from native tyranny, whereas the Russian Empire stretches away into the depths of Asia, and relies on an army largely recruited from amongst many millions of barbarians who have not yet felt the first softening influence of civilization. German thought is abreast of the best in the world; German influences have shaped for good the hopes of the world, but the thought and the hopes of the best in Russia were but the other day drowned in blood by Russia's worst.

To help Britain is to help Russia to the dominance of Europe, to help the barbarian to crush the scientist. That is the reflection of the wise revolutionist of to-day.

Meanwhile the Orange enemy of Irish freedom wisely stays at home and conserves his forces, and the Irish Nationalist is encouraged by his leaders to rush abroad and shed his blood in a quarrel not his own, the simplest elements of which he does not understand.

(*Irish Worker*, August 22nd, 1914.)

A WAR FOR CIVILIZATION!

WE are hearing and reading a lot just now about a war for civilization. In some vague, ill-defined manner we are led to believe that the great empires of Europe have suddenly been seized with a chivalrous desire to right the wrongs of mankind, and have sallied forth to war, giving their noblest blood and greatest treasures to the task of furthering the cause of civilization.

It seems unreal, but it may be possible great emotions sometimes master the most cold and calculating individuals, pushing them on to do that which in their colder moments they would have sneered at. In like manner great emotions sometimes master whole communities of men and women, and nations have gone mad, as in the Crusades, over matters that did not enter into any scheme of selfish calculation.

But in such cases the great emotions manifested themselves in at least an appropriate manner. Their actions under the influence of great emotions had a relation to the cause or the idea for which they were ostensibly warring.

In the case of the War for Civilization, however, we look in vain for any action which in itself bears the mark of civilization. As we count civilization it means the ascendency of industry and the arts of industry over the reign of violence and pillage. Civilization means the conquest by ordered law and peaceful discussion of the forces of evil; it means the exaltation of those whose strength is only in the righteousness of their cause over those whose power is gained by a ruthless seizing of domination founded on force.

Civilization necessarily connotes the gradual supplanting of the reign of chance and muddling by the forces of order and careful prevision for the future; it means the levelling up of classes, and the initiation of the people into a knowledge and enjoyment of all that tends to soften the natural hardships of life and to make that life refined and beautiful.

But the War for Civilization has done none of those things—aspires to do none of those things. It is primarily a war upon a nation whose chief crime is that it refuses to accept a position of dependence, but insists instead upon organizing its forces so that its people can co-operate with nature in making their lives independent of chance, and independent of the goodwill of others.

The War for Civilization is a war upon a nation which insists upon forging to the front in the arts of civilization, which insists upon organizing its intellect so as to produce the highest and best in science, in art, in music, in industry, and insists moreover upon so co-ordinating and linking up all these that the final result shall be a perfectly educated nation of men and women.

In the past, civilization has been a heritage enjoyed by a few upon a basis of the brutalization of the vast multitude; that nation aims at a civilization of the whole resting upon the whole, and only made possible by the educated co-operation of an educated whole.

The War for Civilization is waged by a nation like Russia, which has the greatest proportion of illiterates of any European Power, and which strives sedulously to prevent education where it is possible, and to poison it where prohibition is impossible.

The War for Civilization is waged by a nation like England, which holds in thrall a sixth of the human race[1], and holds as a cardinal doctrine of its faith that none of its subject races may, under penalty of imprisonment and death, dream of ruling their own territories; a nation which believes that all races are subject to purchase, and which brands as perfidy the act of any nation which, like Bulgaria, chooses to carry its wares and its arms to any other than an English market.

This War for Civilization in the name of neutrality and small nationalities invades Persia and Greece, and in the name of the interests of commerce seizes the cargo of neutral ships, and flaunts its defiance of neutral flags.

In the name of freedom from militarism it establishes military rule in Ireland; battling for progress it abolishes trial by jury; and waging war for enlightened rule it tramples the freedom of the Press under the heel of a military despot.

Is it any wonder, then, that this particular War for Civilization arouses no enthusiasm in the ranks of the toiling masses of the Irish nation?

But there is another war for civilization in which these masses are interested. That war is being waged by the forces of organized Labour.

Civilization cannot be built upon slaves; civilization cannot be secured if the producers are sinking

[1] *As a result* of the first World War, 73,000,000 human beings were "acquired" by British Imperialism, which now "holds in thrall" *almost a quarter* of the human race! (Figures for 1932.)

into misery; civilization is lost if they whose labour makes it possible share so little of its fruits that its fall can leave them no worse than its security.

The workers are at the bottom of civilized society. That civilization may endure they ought to push upward from their poverty and misery until they emerge into the full sunlight of freedom. When the fruits of civilization, created by all, are enjoyed in common by all then civilization is secure. Not till then.

Since this European war started, the workers as a whole have been sinking. It is not merely that they have lost in comfort—have lost a certain standard of food and clothing by reason of the increase of prices—but they have lost in a great measure, in England at least, all those hard-won rights of combination, of freedom of action, the possession of which was the foundation upon which they hoped to build the greater freedom of the future.

From being citizens with rights, the workers are being driven and betrayed into the position of slaves with duties. Some of them may have been well-paid slaves, but slavery is not measured by the amount of oats in the feeding trough to which the slave is tied; it is measured by his loss of control of the conditions under which he labours.

We here in Ireland, particularly those who follow the example of the Transport Union, have been battling to preserve those rights which others have surrendered. We have fought to keep up our standards of life, to force up our wages, to better our conditions.

To that extent we have truly been engaged in a war for civilization. Every victory we have gained has gone to increase the security of life amongst our class, has gone to put bread on the tables, coals in the fires, clothes on the backs of those to whom food and warmth and clothing are things of ever-pressing moment.

Some of our class have fought in Flanders and the Dardanelles; the greatest achievement of them all combined will weigh but a feather in the balance for good compared with the achievements of those who stayed at home and fought to secure the rights of the working class against invasion.

The carnival of murder on the Continent will be remembered as a nightmare in the future, will not have the slightest effect in deciding for good the fate of our homes, our wages, our hours, our conditions. But the victories of Labour in Ireland will be as footholds, secure and firm, in the upward climb of our class to the fulness and enjoyment of all that Labour creates and organized society can provide.

Truly, Labour alone in these days is fighting the real WAR FOR CIVILIZATION.

(*The Workers' Republic*, October 30th, 1915.)

THE FRIENDS OF SMALL NATIONALITIES

AS we go to press the "war upon behalf of small nationalities" is still going merrily on in the newspapers. That great champion of oppressed races, Russia, is pouring her armies into East Prussia and Austria and offering freedom and deliverance to all and sundry if they will only take up arms on her behalf —without undue delay; she to be the judge after the war as to whether they did or did not delay unduly. Up to the present it is impossible to find out whether the oppressed races in Europe have or have not risen to the bait.

In our issue of August 22nd[1] I ventured to suggest the probable attitude of the Jews in America towards the appeal of the Russian Czar, that Russian Czar who now styles them "my beloved Jews," and but the other day instructed his agents to organize Jew-hunts and outrages. The correctness of my forecast is now borne out by extracts which the *Gaelic American* reprints from Jewish papers in New York. To help in the good work of educating the people of this country to a correct understanding of the issues at stake in this war, and of the character of the principal actors, I take the liberty of quoting from these reprints, all the more readily as they so amply confirm my own estimate of probabilities.

In the midst of the hustling life of the United States they still remain keenly alive to the struggles of the

[1] See article "America and Europe," p. 43.

old countries, and actively interested in their struggles. Though it may be said that the Jews have no real country, yet it is well to recollect that Austro-Hungary and Russia contain the great majority of the Jews of the world, and that, therefore, they are such a numerically influential portion of the populations of these countries that their attitude in the event of war cannot but be a serious factor. What that attitude is in Russia can only be guessed at from the attitude of those who, living in America, have a freedom of speech impossible to those living under the iron rule of the Czar and his ministers.

The leading Jewish paper in New York—and New York is the greatest Jewish city in the world—is the *Tageblatt*. In its issue of August 5th, it says:

> "What have the Russians, Poles, Bulgarians or Serbians ever done for civilization? They have devised neither political systems nor new ideas. They have simply been imitators. They are experts in fomenting massacres upon unarmed and innocent people. We are all well acquainted with Russia's inhumanity. The Serbians murdered their own King and Queen. The barbarity of the Bulgarians is proved by the report of the Peace Commission. It is quite evident, therefore, that the parasites and assassins of civilization have declared war upon a more enlightened and civilized people. No greater calamity could befall the civilized world than the success of these nations in the present war. A Slavic victory would be a death-blow to progressiveness, democracy, idealism, and free thought; it would destroy the progress of the world in the last hundred years and, in addition, the progress of civilization would be retarded for a long time in the future."

Let the reader remember that the new world, whilst it unites all its immigrants in loyalty to America, does not divest them of the racial antipathies which form part of their European inheritance.

The *Warheit*, a Jewish daily paper, published in Yiddish and exercising an enormous influence upon the advanced Jewish element, as well as upon the working class Jews of all the eastern States, puts the question thus:

> "The question is, on what side must we Jews sympathize? Where do our interests lie? The very question suggests the answer. At the present time, there are only three nations in the whole of Europe whose people are not entirely antagonistic to the Jews. These countries are Austria-Hungary, Germany, and Italy. Never have they been so much hated, persecuted, and despoiled in any countries as in Russia, Roumania, and Greece. It is unfortunate that the Jews in Russia are tied down. Those responsible for the war should be punished, but as long as the war exists it ceases to be a war of monarchs, but one of people, and in that conflict, as Austria-Hungary and Germany have been friendly with the Jews in the past, gratitude requires that they should sympathize with them in the present crisis. Russia has and always will be anti-Semitic. Roumania has treated the Jews like dogs. The Jews have been persecuted in Greece, and even the English have lately begun to hate and persecute the Jews, while in France even their household life is made unbearable. All these considerations naturally incline us to one side. Cursing those who have now compelled Jew to fight Jew, and war in general, we hope and pray that the Austrian and German arms will be victorious in the struggle."

Add to this testimony the fact that the Russian Socialists have issued a strong manifesto denouncing the war, and pouring contempt upon the professions of the Czar in favour of oppressed races, pointing out his suppression of the liberties of Finland, his continued martyrdom of Poland, his atrocious tortures and massacres in the Baltic Provinces, and his withdrawal of the recently granted parliamentary liberties of Russia,[1] and to that again add the fact that the Polish Nationalists have warned the Poles against putting any faith in a man who has proven himself incapable of keeping his solemnly pledged faith with his own people, and you will begin to get a saner view of the great game that is being played than you can ever acquire from the lying Press of Ireland and England.

Of course, that should not blind you to the splendid stand which the British Government, we are assured, is making against German outrages and brutality and in favour of small nationalities. The Russian Government is admitted by every publicist in England to be a foul blot upon civilization. It was but the other day that when the Russian Duma was suppressed by force and many of its elected representatives imprisoned and exiled, an English Cabinet Minister defiantly declared in public, in spite of international courtesies:

"The Duma is dead! Long live the Duma!"

But all that is forgotten now, and the Russian Government and the British Government stand solidly together in favour of small nationalities everywhere except in countries now under Russian and British rule.

[1] See footnote to p. 38.

Yes, I seem to remember a small country called Egypt, a country that through ages of servitude has painfully evolved to a conception of national freedom, and under leaders of its own choosing essayed to make that conception a reality. And I think I remember how this British friend of small nationalities bombarded its chief seaport, invaded and laid waste its territory, slaughtered its armies, imprisoned its citizens, led its chosen leaders away in chains, and reduced the new-born Egyptian nation into a conquered, servile British province.

And I think I remember how, having murdered this new-born soul of nationality amongst the Egyptian people, it signalized its victory by the ruthless hanging at Henshawai of a few helpless peasants who dared to think their pigeons were not made for the sport of British officers.

Also, if my memory is not playing me strange tricks, I remember reading of a large number of small nationalities in India, whose evolution towards a more perfect civilization in harmony with the genius of their race was ruthlessly crushed in blood, whose lands were stolen, whose education was blighted, whose women were left to the brutal lusts of the degenerate soldiery of the British Raj.

Over my vision comes also grim remembrances of two infant republics in South Africa, and I look on the map in vain for them to-day. I remember that the friend of small nationalities waged war upon them—a war of insolent aggression at the instance of financial bloodsuckers. Britain sent her troops to subjugate them, to wipe them off the map; and although they resisted until the veldt ran red with British and Boer blood, the end of the war saw two small nationalities less in the world.

When I read the attempts of the prize Irish Press to work up feeling against the Germans by talk of German outrages at the front, I wonder if those who swallow such yarns ever remember the facts about the exploits of the British generals in South Africa. When we are told of the horrors of Louvain, when the only damage that was done was the result of civilians firing upon German troops from buildings which these troops had in consequence to attack, I remember that in South Africa Lord Roberts issued an order that whenever there was an attack upon the railways in his line of communication every Boer house and farmstead within a radius of ten square miles had to be destroyed.

When I hear of the unavoidable killing of civilians in a line of battle 100 miles long in a densely populated country, being, as it were, part of the German plan of campaign, I remember how the British swept up the whole non-combatant Boer population into concentration camps, and kept it there until the little children died in thousands of fever and cholera; so that the final argument in causing the Boers to make peace was the fear that at the rate of infant mortality in those concentration camps there would be no new generation left to inherit the republic for which their elders were fighting.

This vicious and rebellious memory of mine will also recur to the recent attempt of Persia to form a constitutional government, and it recalls how, when that ancient nation shook off the fetters of its ancient despotism, and set to work to elaborate the laws and forms in the spirit of a modern civilized representative state, Russia, which in solemn treaty with England had guaranteed its independence, at once invaded it, and, slaughtering all its patriots, pillaging its towns and villages, annexed part of its territories, and made the rest a mere Russian dependency. I remember how Sir Edward Grey,[1] who now gushes over the sanctity of treaties, when appealed to to stand by and make Russia stand by the treaty guaranteeing the independence of Persia, coolly refused to interfere.

Oh, yes, they are great fighters for small nationalities, great upholders of the sanctity of treaties!

And the Irish Home Rule Press knows this, knows all these things that a poor workman like myself remembers, knows them all, and is cowardly and guiltily silent, and viciously and fiendishly evil.

Let us hope that all Ireland will not some day have to pay an awful price for the lying attacks of the Home Rule Press upon the noble German nation.

Let our readers encourage and actively spread every paper, circular, leaflet, or manifesto which in those dark days dares to tell the truth.

Thus our honour may be saved; thus the world may learn that the Home Rule Press is but a sewer-pipe for the pouring of English filth upon the shores of Ireland.

(*Irish Worker*, September 12th, 1914.)

[1] Then British Foreign Minister.

THE WAR UPON THE GERMAN NATION

NOW that the first drunkenness of the war fever is over, and the contending forces are locked in deadly combat upon the battlefield, we may expect that the sobering effect of the reports from the front will help to restore greater sanity to the minds of the people. There are thousands of Irish homes to-day from which, deluded by the foolish declaration of Mr. Redmond that Ireland was at one with the Empire in this struggle, and the still more foolish and criminal war-whoops of the official Home Rule Press, there went forth sons and fathers to recruit in the armies of England. If to those thousands of Irish homes from which the call of Mr. Redmond drew forth young Irishmen we add the tens of thousands of homes from which reservists were drawn, we have a vast number of Irish homes in which from this day forward gibbering fear and heart-breaking anxiety will be constantly present—for ever present at the fireside, unbidden guests at the table, loathsome spectres in the darkness grinning from the pillows and the coverlet.

Each day some one of those homes, some days thousands of those homes, will be stricken from the field of battle, and news will come home that this young son or that loving father has met his doom, and out there under a foreign sky the mangled remains, twisted, blown and gashed by inconceivable wounds will lie, each of them in all their ghastly horror crying out to

Heaven for vengeance upon the political tricksters who lured them to their fate.

Poor and hunger-harassed as are the members of the Irish Transport Workers' Union, is there one of them who to-day has not a happier position and a clearer conscience than the so-called leaders of the Irish race, who are responsible for deluding into enlisting to fight England's battles the thousands of Irish youths whose corpses will ere many months be manuring the soil of a foreign country, or whose mangled bodies will be contemptuously tossed home to starve—a burden and a horror to all their kith and kin?

Read this report from the *Daily News and Leader* of the 25th inst. of the statement of an Alsatian peasant who saw some of the fighting in Alsace. He says:

> "The effects of artillery fire are terrific. The shells burst, and where you formerly saw a heap of soldiers you then see a heap of corpses, or a number of figures writhing on the ground, torn and mutilated by the exploded fragments."

And when you have read that then think of the many thousands of our boys—for, God help us and them, they are still our brave Irish boys though deluded into fighting for the oppressor—around whom such shells will be falling by day and by night for many a long month to come. Think of them, and think also of the multitude of brave German boys who never did any harm to them or to us, but who rather loved us and our land, and our tongue and our ancient literature, and consider that those boys of ours will be busy sending shot and shell and rifle ball into their midst, murdering and mangling German lives and limbs, widowing humble German women, orphaning helpless German children.

Such reflections will perhaps open the way for the more sane frame of mind I spoke of at the beginning of this article. To help in clarifying the thought of our people that such sanity may be fruitful in greater national as well as individual wisdom, permit me, then, to present a few facts to those whose attitude upon the war has so far been determined by the criminal jingoism of the daily Press. I wish to try and trace *the real origin of this war upon the German nation*, for despite all the truculent shouts of a venal Press and conscienceless politicians, this war is not a war upon German militarism, but upon the industrial activity of the German nation.

If the reader were even slightly acquainted with the history of industry in Europe he would know that as a result of the discovery of steam as a motive power, and the consequent development of machine industry depending upon coal, Great Britain towards the close of the eighteenth century began to dominate the commercial life of the world. Her large coal supply helped her to this at a time when the coal supply of other countries had not yet been discovered or exploited. Added to this was the fact that the ruling class of England by a judicious mixing in European struggles, by a dexterous system of alliances, and a thoroughly unscrupulous use of her sea power, was able to keep the Continent continually embroiled in war whilst her own shores were safe. Whilst the cities and towns of other countries were constantly the prey of rival armies, their social life crushed under the cannon wheels of contending forces, and their brightest young men compelled to give to warfare the intellect that might have enriched their countries by industrial achievements, England was able peacefully to build up her industries, to spread her wings of commerce, and to become the purveyor-general of manufactured goods to the civilized and uncivilized nations of the world. In her own pet phrase she was "the workshop of the world," and other nations were but as so many agricultural consumers of the products of England's factories and workshops.

Obviously such a state of matters was grossly artificial and unnatural. It could not be supposed by reasonable men that the civilized nations would be content to remain for ever in such a condition of tutelage or dependence. Rather was it certain that self-respecting nations would begin to realize that the industrial overlordship by England of Europe meant the continued dependence of Europe upon England—a most humiliating condition of affairs.

So other nations began quietly to challenge the unquestioned supremacy of England in the markets. They began first to produce for themselves what they had hitherto relied upon England to produce for them, and passed on from that to enter into competition with English goods in the markets of the world. Foremost and most successful European nation in this endeavour to escape from the thraldom of dependence upon England's manufactures stands the German nation. To this contest in the industrial world it brought all the resources of science and systematized effort. Early learning that an uneducated people is necessarily an inferior people, the German nation attacked the work of educating its children with such success that it is now universally admitted that the Germans are the best educated people in Europe. Basing its industrial effort upon an educated working class, it accomplished in the workshop results that this half-educated working class of England could only wonder at. That English working class, trained to a slavish subservience to rule-of-thumb methods, and under managers welded to traditional processes, saw themselves gradually out-classed by a new rival in whose service were enrolled the most learned scientists co-operating with the most educated workers in mastering each new problem as it arose, and unhampered by old traditions, old processes, or old equipment. In this fruitful marriage of science and industry the Germans were pioneers, and if it seemed that in starting both they became unduly handicapped it was soon realized that if they had much to learn they had at least nothing to unlearn, whereas the British remained hampered at every step by the accumulated and obsolete survivals of past industrial competitions.

Despite the long hold that England had upon industry, despite their pre-emption of the market, despite the influence of their far-flung empire, German competition became more and more a menace to England's industrial supremacy; more and more German goods took the place of English. Some few years ago the cry of "Protection" was raised in England in the hopes that English trade would be thus saved by a heavy customs duty against imported commodities. But it was soon realized that as England was chiefly an exporting country a tax upon imported goods would not save her industrial supremacy. From the moment that realization entered into the minds of the British capitalist we may date the inception of this war.

It was determined that since Germany could not be beaten in fair competition industrially, she must be beaten unfairly by organizing a military and naval conspiracy against her. British methods and British capitalism might be inferior to German methods and German capitalism; German scientists aided by German workers might be superior to British workers and tardy British science; but the British fleet was still superior to the German in point of numbers and weight of artillery. Hence it was felt that if the German nation could be ringed round with armed foes upon its every frontier until the British fleet could strike at its ocean-going commerce, then German competition would be crushed and the supremacy of England in commerce ensured for another generation. The conception meant calling up the forces of barbaric power to crush and hinder the development of the peaceful powers of industry. It was a conception worthy of fiends, but what do you expect? You surely do not expect the roses of honour and civilization to grow on the thorn tree of capitalist competition—and that tree planted in the soil of a British ruling class.

But what about the independence of Belgium? Aye, what about it?

Remember that the war found England thoroughly prepared, Germany totally unprepared. That the British fleet was already mobilized on a scale never attempted in times of peace, and the German fleet was scattered in isolated units all over the seven seas. That all the leading British commanders were at home ready for the emergency, and many German and

Austrian officers, such as Slatin Pasha, have not been able to get home yet. Remember all this and realize how it reveals that the whole plan was ready prepared; and hence that the cry of "Belgium" was a mere subterfuge to hide the determination to crush in blood the peaceful industrial development of the German nation. Already the British Press is chuckling with joy over the capture of German trade. All capitalist journals in England boast that the Hamburg-American Line will lose all its steamers, valued at twenty millions sterling. You know what that means! It means that a peaceful trade, built up by peaceful methods, is to be struck out of the hands of its owners by the sword of an armed pirate. You remember the words of John Mitchel[1] descriptive of the British Empire as "a pirate empire, robbing and plundering upon the high seas."

Understand the game that is afoot, the game that Christian England is playing, and when next you hear apologists for capitalism tell of the wickedness of Socialists in proposing to "confiscate" property, remember the plans of British and Irish capitalists to steal German trade—the fruits of German industry and German science.

Yes, friends, Governments in capitalist society are but committees of the rich to manage the affairs of the capitalist class. The British capitalist class has planned this colossal crime in order to ensure its uninterrupted domination of the commerce of the world. To achieve that end it is prepared to bathe a continent in blood,

[1] An Irish revolutionary Nationalist who had connections with the Fenian movement. His writings earned him imprisonment and banishment. These punishments broke his health and, although returned by the electors of Tipperary in 1875, he died a month later.

to kill off the flower of the manhood of the three most civilized great nations of Europe, to place the iron heel of the Russian tyrant upon the throat of all liberty-loving races and peoples from the Baltic to the Black Sea, and to invite the blessing of God upon the spectacle of the savage Cossack ravishing the daughters of a race at the head of Christian civilization.

Yes, this war is the war of a pirate upon the German nation.

And up from the blood-soaked graves of the Belgian frontiers the spirits of murdered Irish soldiers of England call to Heaven for vengeance upon the parliamentarian tricksters who seduced them into the armies of the oppressor of their country.

(*Irish Worker*, August 29th, 1914.)

SOME PERVERTED BATTLE LINES

NOTHING is more remarkable in this war than the manner in which the ruling class in the countries of the Triple Alliance have appropriated and used for their own purposes every phrase and rallying cry that their political opponents had coined against them. For years the Socialists have preached against war,[1] and preached with such vehemence and argumentative persuasiveness that their anti-militarist campaign had profoundly influenced public opinion in Europe, and raised hopes that the era of international blood-letting was past. Vain delusion! As soon as the capitalist class of England concluded that the time was ripe for the destruction of their German competitors, so far from finding the peace campaign of the Socialists a hindrance, it proceeded to use it as a useful asset in the militarist business. With perfectly fiendish and sardonic humour it took up the rallying cries of the Peace Party and used them as its very own. It called upon the Labour Parties, the Socialists, the humanitarians among the Liberals and Radicals to rally to

[1] At Stuttgart (1907), Copenhagen (1910) and Basle (1912) the International Socialist Congress solemnly agreed that their constituent Socialist parties would do their utmost to prevent the outbreak of imperialist war. Should they be unsuccessful in this, they resolved to oppose any such war and to make use of the crisis caused by that war to overthrow capitalism. Compare this with the Hastings Conference of the Labour Party (1933) resolution, pledging the Party "to take no part in war and to resist it with the whole force of the Labour movement . . . including a General Strike." To-day members of the Labour Party Executive who welcomed this resolution are in the Cabinet of the Coalition Government. Furthermore, they agree with the Tories that strikes of any kind should be illegal.

the aid of the British Army to "make war upon war," to "put an end to militarism," to "bring peace on earth and goodwill among men" at the point of British bayonets, and to sweep German commerce off the seas as a preliminary to establishing brotherhood with the German peoples. With the honourable exceptions of the Independent Labour Party[1] and the Socialist Labour Party, the organized and unorganized Labour advocates of peace in Great Britain swallowed the bait, and are now beating the war-drums and hounding their brothers on to the butchery of their German comrades—and hounding them on with the cant of fraternity on their lips.

For a generation the French Government has made war upon the secular power of the Catholic Church in France. It abolished the Concordat between Church and State, made public property of the churches, did away with religious teaching in its schools, removed all religious emblems from its courts of law and public buildings, seized and auctioned off property the Church claimed as its own, and exercised its power with such relentlessness that many religious orders abandoned the country and removed themselves and all their belongings to Ireland, America, Belgium and other more friendly countries. Whether it was in its right or not is immaterial—the material point is that in its defence the Church through all its organs represented France as a godless, atheistical country which God in His own good time would doubtless punish in order to avenge His persecuted faithful.

[1] The I.L.P. was forced into this position by its purely pacifist attitude, which later was one cause of its denunciation of Connolly's revolutionary struggle in 1916.

But when it became necessary to go to war with Germany, France joined England in raising a newspaper wail over the sufferings of "poor Catholic Belgium," planted machine guns in the churches at Louvain and field artillery before the Cathedral at Rheims, and when the Germans in self-defence trained their own artillery upon these sacred buildings in order to destroy the French fire the resultant damage was made the basis of an allegation that the Germans were making war upon religion which the pious French Government were nobly defending. To aid this business of representing this French Government as noble crusaders in defence of the Catholic faith, hundreds of little Belgian children have been deported to Great Britain and Ireland, and are now being scattered up and down the land so Catholics may be moved by sympathy with their suffering to go out and fight for the French Government, which a few months ago they were being taught to curse in the name of Catholicity.

Just as the peace campaign in England became a weapon in the hands of the War Party, so the Catholic propaganda in Ireland and England has been made a valuable tool in the services of the free-thinking rulers of France.

The small, conquered nations of Europe have in a thousand ways fought to propagate the idea of nationality, to emphasize the value of small nations and their special contributions to civilization. Part and parcel of their propaganda has of necessity been directed against those two Empires which in Europe stand alone in the unenviable position of suppressing national existences and insisting upon small nations conforming to the mould in which these empires would cast them. But as soon as these two empires, England and Russia—the only two empires in Europe, we repeat, which do not respect the existence of small nations within their borders[1]—as soon as England and Russia go to war they, with the effrontery of a Satan, raise the slogans of small nationalities as their battle cries, and call upon the world to admire them as the deliverers of the oppressed nations.

And to crown all, we see Ireland, which for centuries has whined to Europe for relief against England, now being led by its elected leader to fight for England, that the British Empire might continue to keep its navy as a sword at the throat of Europe.

The irony of it all!

(*Irish Worker*, September 26th, 1914.)

[1] In the original text this passage reads: "the only two empires in Europe, we repeat, which do not respect the formation of small empires within their borders." This is an obvious slip either on the part of the *Irish Worker* printer or of Connolly himself and I have taken the liberty of correcting it.—P. M.

WAR AT HOME

THE war is still dragging its weary way along. On Saturday the Allies captured 3 yards, 2 feet and 7 inches, and on Sunday the Germans recaptured 3 yards, 1 foot and 11 inches. Thus it is easy to calculate how long it will take us to get to Berlin.

The war at home is also making great progress. Every Monday the landlords' forces make a successful dash upon the entrenchments of the enemy in the tenement houses of Dublin, and come away laden with spoil, leaving behind them a motley array of rent books and notices to quit.

On the same day mounted forces of the Shilling-a-Week Brigade descend in relentless raids upon the homes of the poor, and poor women and children can be seen rushing in droves to the pawnbrokers for ammunition to satisfy the raiders.

In addition to these continual charges upon the entrenchments of the poor, large forces of the enemy are at all times busy in intercepting our convoys of food, and from their strategic positions in the bakery and provision shops are able by increasing prices to spread hunger and misery in the ranks of the workers. Up to the present all counter-attacks have failed to dislodge them, although serious food riots are reported from England.

The Transport Union has successfully led several attacks upon the enemy, and has captured a large number of War Bonuses and other military material.

But not being properly supported by others, the attack was not carried farther into the enemy's entrenchments, with the result that, although the Transport Union kept the position it won, the other portions of the forces of Labour are still struggling in an attempt to secure the necessary supplies.

In addition to this, great masses of the Workers, being unorganized and therefore undisciplined, are still lying helpless outside the barbed wire entanglements of the Good Pirates.

The workers in Cork are still lying around helpless waiting for some great leader to come along and save them. Generally in the past they sacrificed the leader after he had saved them, so in the present case there is no great desire on anybody's part to do the saving act.

The dock labourers of Cork, like the dock labourers of Waterford and some other places, have not yet risen to a realization of the dignity of their class. Their one thought is to get some one to help them, to do something for them, and then when they have reaped that benefit they look for the first opportunity to find fault with the organization which secured the benefit for them.

They have not been able to realize that only in organization can men win rights, and only by still more organization can they keep those rights. They do not seem to grasp the fact that better homes and better life, like all the good things of the world, must be paid for, and that organization is the price that the labourer must pay.

The men who in each place have stood by the Union are the men who keep up the standard of wages for all. They are the men in the gap of danger. Upon their existence and courage rests the hope of Labour. To them is due the fact that the various hosts of the capitalist enemy have been prevented from swallowing up again all the hard-won gains of the workers of Ireland.

Let them stand to their posts, stand undaunted and watching until the shameful deserters crawl back to the army and the fort they abandoned; until the workers throughout Ireland once more fall in behind the splendid hosts of the Dublin fighters in the battle for industrial freedom.

For industrial freedom; aye, and the battle for industrial freedom breeds true and sterling fighters for the freedom of the nation. Should the red tide of battle ever flow in Ireland the first of Ireland's ranks will be those who knew how to build and organize for Labour; just as true as it is that they who will first desert Ireland for a foreign flag will be those who first deserted the flag of Labour.

In case the Germans should ever attempt to invade Ireland, it is just as well to inform them that our women workers in the shirtmaking trade are at present agitating for the Trade Board (Ireland) to fix a minimum rate of wages for female workers, other than learners, of 3½d. per hour, and that said Board has invited the employers to send in objections, which may be lodged within three months from May 20th, 1915.

The hoardings are covered with recruiting posters appealing to the "Women of Ireland" to get their boys to enlist. We warn the Germans to beware of the deathless courage of the men who can look on undauntedly whilst these "Women of Ireland" are piteously agitating for a wage of 3½d. per hour.

The sufferings of the Belgian children also rise to

our eyes when we learn that the same Board proposes to increase the wages of female learners to 3s. 6d. per week of 50 hours.

Three months' notice to oppose that is also given to the employers, and we are thus left in the dark as to the real rates paid at present. But when we see the rights of the poor employer to purchase Irish flesh and blood at a lower rate than 3s. 6d. per week being thus interfered with, we at once scent the evil hand of the alien enemy. Surely nobody but a German spy would thus strike such a fell blow at our Irish industries.

Where is the Irish employer who would not die in defence of the glorious empire which allows him to make a profit out of the flesh and blood (and tears) of helpless Irish womanhood and girlhood?

Where is he? Why, he is sitting snugly in his office, smoking a cigar, and talking of conscription to force the husbands, fathers and brothers of his female slaves to go out and fight for him!

I take this cutting from the pages of our bright contemporary, the *British Seafaring Journal*:

> "We are told that in the United Kingdom there are close upon 17 million acres of waste land. I should have to tax my memory to recall a single acre of what might be fairly termed 'waste land' in all the many visits I have paid to different parts of Germany. Also with regard to waste of human material the results visible to the naked eye cannot fail to strike the traveller. It is true that statistics disclose an ominously rising average of crime, but the wastrel, the do-nothing, the loafer, those with whose presence we are pestered at home, are rarely to be met with in Germany.
>
> SIDNEY WHITMAN."

If the same could be said of Ireland what a rich country this could be made! For in Ireland the waste land and the waste human material alike exist in riotous profusion. A wise statesman, nay, a benefactor to the race would be he who could bring those two together, that united they might by their co-operation enrich our common country. But in Ireland all the legislative and administrative forces seem to aim at increasing the quantity of both kinds of waste.

Think of it: No waste land, no waste human material in Germany; much waste land, much waste human material in Ireland. What is the moral, the lesson?[1] But I am getting too dangerously near to the Defence of the Realm Act.[2]

The land of Ireland is well intersected with canals which in other countries provide the very cheapest kind of carriage for goods, but the railway companies of Ireland have bought up the canals to prevent them serving the Irish public. Thus the public lose the facilities which the canals would give, and the railways, secure in their monopoly, settle down into a state of slovenly inefficiency which makes them a national scandal. Irish railway companies make no attempt to develop Irish industry, or to develop Irish districts. Rather, they seem to regard themselves as alien enemies, holding a position over a conquered people which

[1] Connolly's efforts to combat Britain's hawking of atrocity stories have sometimes been misinterpreted as a " pro-German " attitude. The best answer to this is the famous streamer which hung outside his headquarters at Liberty Hall: "We serve neither King nor Kaiser, but Ireland."

[2] The Defence of the Realm Act, better known as "Dora," was used during the last war, not only to safeguard military interests, but also to curtail political and Trade Union rights. In the present war it has been revived in its main essentials under the name of the Emergency Powers (Defence) Act.

enables them to compel that people to go on for ever paying a War Indemnity for the mere right to live.

Slovenly in their methods, contemptuous in their dealings with the general public, tyrannical and sweating in their treatment of their workers, the Irish railway companies make us long for the day when an Irish State will assume, in the interest of Ireland, the power and ownership they have exploited so mercilessly for mean and sordid ends.

(*The Workers' Republic*, June 25th, 1915.)

OUR DISAPPEARING LIBERTIES

ONE of the commonplaces of the political orator is the saying that "the price of liberty is eternal vigilance," a saying which implies that the liberties of mankind are continually endangered from the inroads of unscrupulous enemies against whose attacks we must ever be on the alert. It implies also that the normal state of society is a state of war; that mankind, even amongst the most progressive nations, is ever in danger of seeing its painfully acquired liberties wrested from it and fresh chains substituted, and that consequently they who wish to see progress maintained and the bounds of freedom enlarged must be ever on the watch lest upon some specious excuse they lose in a day what their fathers agonized for during generations to win.

This political proverb we seem in peril of forgetting in these troublous times. On every side we see fresh inroads made upon our liberties, but no Irish voice is raised in protest, perhaps no Irish voice dare be raised. But no matter what the risk be, we who essay to voice the hopes and defend the cause of Labour dare not be silent. The needs of the multitude call for expression —it shall not be said they called in vain. If fresh chains are forged for the workers it shall not be said that we by our silence allowed those who trusted us to remain ignorant of the fact that the chains were in preparation.

In the first place we direct attention to the fact that

the meanest and cruellest form of conscription is already in active operation in this country. Without consulting any of them as to their opinions upon the justification or otherwise of this war, employers are every day giving to their employees the intimation that they must choose between enlistment and starvation. It matters not that the employer may himself be young or vigorous, or have sons young and vigorous, whilst the workman may have a family of little children depending upon him: that employer sits smoking in his office chair and orders the helpless wage-slave to don a uniform he hates, or suffer dismissal and starvation. No greater violation of the right of the individual has ever been known to history. When a man is ordered to take a deadly weapon and proceed to kill a human being with whom he believes he has no grounds of quarrel, personal or national, if the fear of starvation makes him obey that order, then the person issuing that command is guilty of the foulest crime known to humanity—the murder of a human soul. Against such an attack upon the liberty of the individual we protest, and call upon all to protest. Conscription is bad, we hate the thought of it, but conscription is at least openly brutal; this conscription by starvation is foul with the foulness of Hell. We are not alone in this belief. There are thousands who believe in the justness of this war who are sickened with loathing of the means taken to obtain soldiers to carry it on.

Throughout Ireland every day we read of prosecutions under the Defence of the Realm Act in which the triviality of the charges is such as is calculated to bring more contempt than respect upon those responsible. For that we do not repine, nor pretend to repine.

But when it appears that the liberty of the most respectable man or woman in this country is absolutely at the mercy of the most disreputable and drunken soldiers that ever disgraced a uniform, it is time to call a halt. In many cases we have seen drunken soldiers deliberately pick quarrels with respectable civilians, and after abusing and ill-treating them call upon the police to arrest those whom they had abused and ill-treated. The police always obey, and the magistrates always convict. On the tram, in the streets, in places of amusement or refreshment, nowadays it is a positive danger to be in the proximity of a soldier. Many of these are decent, cleanly enough, but at any time the lowest amongst them may elect to force his gross conversation upon you, and should you resent, the services of the police are called in and a term of imprisonment is certain.

On Sunday whilst the Labour Day procession was going to the Park one of those rowdies attempted to ride a bicycle right through the thickest ranks of the processionists; others on the ground in the Park endeavoured by ribald language and horseplay to stir up trouble wherever they saw groups of policemen convenient to their activities, but fortunately the demonstrators, strong in the consciousness of their own power, were not moved to active hostility.

We wonder if the governing authorities are really aware of all this. Surely no one can be so fatuous as to imagine that the British Army can be popularized by such methods. If we did believe that this kind of thing had really the support of the Government we should not waste our space in chronicling it; it is because we realize that it may spread upward that we speak ere it be too late. Magistrates and soldiers and policemen and Coalition Cabinets must be made to understand that they all exist in theory for the sake of serving the civilian. If the contrary obtains, if, as seems to be the danger in Ireland, the civilian is subordinated to the soldier, and becomes a dog for all those we have named to kick and abuse, then it will become very difficult indeed to understand wherein lies that constitutional freedom we have lately heard so much about.

The liberty of public meeting is also rapidly becoming a thing of the past in Ireland, as far as it is or may be used for the criticism of the activities of the Government or its functionaries, and yet it is this very right of the subject to criticize the governing bodies which is the very essence of freedom in a constitutionally governed country. Without the freedom of the press and the right of public meeting there is no citizenship, there are only the relations of subject and rulers, of slaves and slave-drivers. The question of whether the Press is or is not wrong in its criticisms, or whether the public meeting does or does not advocate wise measures or use wise language has no bearing upon the matter. The Press criticisms are subject to the judgment of the readers; the public meeting stands or falls with the justice of its cause. To allow either to be judged or punished by those against whom they are directed, is to abolish all constitutional guarantees and to establish the naked rule of force. Against that we protest with all our strength. It is idle to speak of great national emergencies requiring such suppression of liberties. Great national emergencies can only be met by calling upon the reserves of good in our national character, by invoking the aid of all that is best and ennobling. Whatever cause seeks to flourish by stifling criticism and imprisoning thought is a hateful cause, and can only rely upon the support of those natures who turn instinctively to darkness and obscurity.

For all who love the light for the help it brings to the cause of progress the duty is plain. Every one of the liberties our fathers won must be fought for tenaciously! War or no war, none of our hard-won rights should be, or will be, surrendered without a struggle.

(*The Workers' Republic*, June 5th, 1915.)

LIBERTY AND LABOUR

DECIDEDLY we are getting on! Since this war started we have been progressing at a rate calculated to bewilder the mind of the ordinary man or woman. Especially in the direction of freedom our progress has been of quite a giddy character.

First, on the grounds that their activities were calculated to hinder the fight which the Allies were making for liberty, the liberties of the Press were curtailed. And as if to emphasize the great truth(?) that militarism must be crushed, the military were sent in to break up the machinery on which the *Irish Worker* was printed.

Then other papers which ventured to doubt the peaceful intentions and liberty-loving enthusiasm of the British Government were squelched in their turn.

Then certain Irishmen were ordered to leave military districts, and under a kind of ticket-of-leave system report their residence elsewhere. We would not presume, being laymen, to doubt the wisdom of the military authorities, but it does seem a little erratic when you suspect a man of knowing too much to remove him out of your jurisdiction. It would seem safer to keep him under your eye.

Next, trial by jury, that great bulwark of British liberty, went by the board, and we have seen men refused the right of such trial, and summarily sentenced to a long term of imprisonment for expressing opinions upon the war.

In all the great wars of England, the war of the American Revolution, the war against the French Revolution, the Crimean War, there were men who stood out against those ventures, and against a nation lashed to madness by the appeals and lies of its leaders. They were but a miserable minority, but history has triumphantly vindicated them.

They suffered from mob fury, and from legal oppression, but none was condemned and sentenced without a trial by jury. The jury may have been, and was in most cases, composed of bitter partisans of the Government, but it was still a jury. The Government of those days did not dare to destroy the civic rights of its subjects on the pretext of military necessity.

Every one of those men, whose names Englishmen to-day delight to honour for their courage in withstanding the tyrants and demagogues of their day, would now be arrested under the Defence of the Realm Act, as other men have been for "crimes" not a hundredth part as well calculated to "give aid to the enemy."

Now we find that a new office has been created, that of Ministry of Munitions, and we are already told that the Minister in charge will have absolute power over the labour and liberties of the subjects whose labour he requires, or thinks he requires, in the factories, workshops, or shipyards of the nation.

All Trade Union regulations are swept away at once, and swept away, be it remembered, with the connivance of the British Trade Union leaders.[1] It does not seem to matter that those Trade Union regulations are the result of generations of experience of what was necessary to safeguard the lives and health of the workers—they are swept away as ruthlessly as if they were but the idlest speculations of Utopian dreamers.

Yes, we are getting on! Our right of a free Press no longer exists, our right of public meeting is a trap and a peril instead of a safeguard, our sanctity of domicile—the privacy of our homes—is continually violated, our Trade Union rights are going where they have not already gone, and all sections of the master class have instructed the leaders of their political parties to support each other against any criticism from the under dogs.

The Coalition Cabinet is the sign and symbol to all who understand that the ruling classes no longer think it necessary to pretend that great principles divide them.

The Liberal lies down with the Conservative, and the Home Ruler with the leader of the Orange hosts. Home Rule is on the Statute Book, but the chief figure in the new Cabinet is the man who organized 50,000 armed men to resist by force its passage from the position of an Act to that of a fact.[2] Could anything

[1] Compare with to-day; Mr. Bevin, for example, at the Southport T.U.C. (October 9th, 1940): "We have to ask you to agree to what are virtually great restrictions, to give up treasured rights. . . ." If confirmation is required from the enemies of Labour, what about this: "The labour leaders in our present Government are exhibiting a magnificent power of leadership in the furtherance of our war effort, even to the extent of abandoning many cherished Trade Union principles" (from a circular issued by a well-known firm of London stockbrokers and discussed in the *Financial News*, September 10th, 1940).

[2] Sir Edward Carson.

be truer than the following remarks, reported in the daily Press, of Father O'Grady, P.P., Chaplain of the Keash (Co. Sligo) Branch of the A.O.H.?[1]

> "What, Father O'Grady asked, had they got in return? Could the purpose of the Coalition Government be achieved without inflicting a more deadly wound on three-fourths of Ireland's population than a thousand Zeppelins could inflict? Could any more traitorous indignity be offered by 'the sympathetic Government' to loyal and Nationalist Ireland than the appointment of Sir E. Carson, and the proposed appointment of Mr. Campbell—rebels of years' standing—to positions demanding respect for law and order at least to those who hold them? Twelve months ago Home Rule was a certainty; to-day it is dead."

Carson organized an army to fight the forces of the Crown, but now he is one of the men who will direct the armed forces of the Crown to whatever end he and his may desire. Jonah has swallowed the whale.

We are progressing! O, yes, but whither?

Never was it more necessary for the forces of Labour to be alert, watchful and determined. The classes who control these countries are seemingly determined to utilize every opportunity given them in order to further their class interests, quite regardless of how their schemes may injuriously affect the nation at large.

We have seen the monies promised for the work of tearing down the slums and rebuilding Dublin blown away at the cannon's mouth, along with the sums needed to complete the Land Purchase Schemes;

[1] Ancient Order of Hibernians—a Roman Catholic organization in many respects comparable to Freemasonry.

we have seen the war crisis taken advantage of to compel the enforcement upon Ireland of compulsory vaccination without the Conscience Clause that safeguards the English parent; we have seen pliant Labour leaders assisting at the organization of a Dockers Battalion under military law to do work which civilian Trade Union dockers were willing to do, and we have seen members of that battalion subjected to severe military penalties for trifling delays which in civil life would only cause a frown;[1] we have seen an Englishman arrested for mentioning that the King is of German descent—a fact that said Englishman was taught in the public schools of his country. In short we have seen, and are daily seeing, a continual narrowing of the bounds of freedom, a steady increase of the power of a plutocratic State, a silent, relentless invasion of military power upon the domain of civil law and civil rights.

Against such things it behoves all who value freedom and the possibilities of peaceful progress to organize our forces to make a determined stand. In this matter every man's battle is our battle. Every man or woman who takes up a stand for liberty is our comrade, and their cause should be our cause. No petty personal quarrels should count, no question of the rivalry of organizations, no foolish strivings after exclusive credit for any man or any party. In this battle, the lines of which are now being traced, it will be the duty of every lover of the country and of the race to forget all minor dividing lines and issues, and in contemplating

[1] To-day the Pioneers (tradesmen, etc., "under military law") are at work clearing the streets of debris after air raids for 2s. 6d. per day while able-bodied trade unionists are unemployed. Conscripted craftsmen are also driving railway engines, doing municipal plumbing, etc.

the work before us to seek earnestly after the unity of the progressive forces.

Labour must be the backbone of all the resistance to tyranny. Labour has won a few steps forward and upward, but it has a long and weary climb before it—a climb so long and weary that it cannot afford to lose a single one of the liberties it has already gained.

Already our eyes have been gladdened by the sight of that rally, and from all over Ireland comes the answering shout of joy at the sight. The heart of the nation is good and sound, the courage of the workers not abated one whit.

We are living in perilous times. But we shall not flinch from the struggle.

(*The Workers' Republic*, June 19th, 1915.)

GOD HELP THE POOR IRISH

TO all thoughtful Labour men and women the recent meeting of the British Trade Union Congress presented a rather sorrowful spectacle. Time was when that Congress was regarded as embodying all the bright hopes and aspirations of a working class rapidly freeing itself from the mental and political fetters inherited from ages of servitude. Time was when the most beloved spokesmen of that Congress were those who most passionately declared that it was the duty of the workers to overthrow all the social, political and military tyrannies rooted in the capitalist system of which the British Empire is the perfected fruit. Time was when the unanimous voice of that Congress declared that the working class had no enemy except the capitalist class—that of its own country at the head of the list. Time was when the orators at all the meetings attendant upon that Congress declaimed their love of human brotherhood, and their contempt for all the racial, religious and national catch cries that were used to keep the peoples separate and warring.

But now! Alas, how have the mighty fallen! Gone are all the bright hopes of a class fighting to free itself from fetters, and scornfully contemptuous of the interests or ambitions of its masters. Instead, we have a Congress deliberately putting aside the hopes of the workers in order to help the schemes of murder set on foot by the capitalist state. We have a Congress where a leader like George N. Barnes uses his position to attack his own Union for insisting upon its Trade Union rights;[1] where a leader like the President of the Congress advises his hearers not to read literature presenting a different view on the war to that popularized by the capitalist newspapers;[2] where a leader like Ben Tillet foams at the mouth against those who desire peace as a few months ago he foamed at the mouth against those who desired war; where every voice belched forth hatred of their brothers under a different government,[3] and where the quarrels fomented by the capitalist class were made more important as standards of worth than services in the interests of Labour, or aspirations for a world where men can live guiltless of plotting the murder of their fellow-men. A Congress which declared against compulsory service or conscription, but in the same breath declared it would accept it if its rulers declared it to be necessary.

We have ere now looked hopefully to the British Trade Union Congress, but our hopes are gone. The British Empire is ruled by the most astute ruling class in the world; the British working

[1] Sir Walter Citrine, of course, has more recently (1940) signed a circular advising Labour organizations to have nothing to do with the National Council for Civil Liberties, a non-party organization struggling to defend the rights of the individual !

[2] The President of a more recent Congress (Southport, October, 1940) secured the expulsion from the Congress of the *Daily Worker* reporters on political grounds. Full facilities were naturally given to the capitalist Press.

[3] And here is how Labour leader Mr. Bevin belches forth hatred (Stockport again): "We have been urged by people to hit back. Yes, we'll do it. An eye for an eye, if you like, but we must have the bombers, the arms and the Navy. Force is the only language the Nazis understand."

class is the most easily fooled working class in the world.

God help the poor Irish as long as they remain yoked to such a combination.

(*The Workers' Republic*, September 18th, 1915.)

THE RIGHT TO STRIKE

WE would advise all interested in the peaceful development of the Labour Movement to watch carefully the progress of events in connection with the activities of the Minister for Munitions. It will be noted that in his negotiations with the British Labour leaders this wily Welshman has already succeeded in inducing a very large section of these gentlemen to surrender the "right to strike," on behalf of the workers they represent. This means that in the industries in which their members are interested the workers have surrendered the only weapon they possess of immediate effective value in compelling a hearing for their demands. We have not yet heard of any corresponding surrender on the part of the employers—have not heard of the capitalist class giving up any of the power they possess over the lives of their employees. It is only the workers who are asked to surrender civic rights—rights hard won by generations of fighters. It will of course be argued that this is for the war only. Even if that be so it cannot be cited as a justification for the surrender; it may be used as an argument against the war. For if the war can only be pursued by virtue of robbing from the civil population all the privileges hitherto enjoyed by them, then no friend of freedom and orderly progress can fail to be opposed to the war. But upon what guarantee is the statement based that this denial of the right to strike will not persist after the war? Do we not all know that the world after the war will be mightily changed, that many institutions are being introduced as war measures that will be carried over into times of peace ? He would indeed be foolish who did not realize that each innovation which we see being introduced into the industrial world will, if it proves effective for its present progress, become an established fact too difficult to dislodge when war is over.[1]

Our friends who say that the denial of the right to strike is only a war measure would do well to study out the processes by which it can be justified on that ground. They will find that every argument that can be used to justify that denial now, can easily be stretched to justify similar restrictions in time of peace. For instance, what is the argument that made it necessary in war-time? The answer is that such restriction is necessary in the interests of national self-preservation. Well, what is to prevent the ruling class saying hereafter that any strike in a basic industry, such as the transport, the railway, the mines, the engineering, is a menace to the well-being of the nation, and that therefore it ought to be prohibited in the interests of national self-preservation ? There is nothing to prevent them doing so, but much self-interest impelling them to such action.

And any tyro in politics knows that Great Britain above all countries in the world is governed by precedent. If it can be proven in a British Court of Law that any particular decision was once given before and accepted as Law, then the judge of that Court will give his decision exactly on similar lines, though it

[1] Connolly's suspicions were justified. Restrictions of the right to strike lingered on under the name of the Trades Disputes Act.

may involve the most manifest absurdity and heinous injustice. Hence this denial of the right to strike is full of dangers for the future, and the British Labour leaders in accepting it have grossly betrayed the class to which they belong, or did belong.

Thus another liberty is disappearing. Already we have seen trial by jury destroyed in Ireland, as in the cases of Sean Milroy and Sheehy Skeffington; we have seen the Crown arresting a man in one part of the country and arbitrarily fixing his trial to take place in another, as in the case of Sean Mac Diarmada, and we have seen newspapers suppressed, type stolen and machinery dismantled by the orders of the Government, which at the same time refused to specify any one article, paragraph, or sentence in these papers upon which the confiscation and suppression was based.[1]

Now we see that the right of the workers to withhold their labour is also taken away. Every worker under these regulations is bound to labour when and where he is told, and if he does not like the conditions he is graciously allowed to grumble, but grumble he as much as he chooses he must keep on working under the conditions against which he is grumbling. This is freedom as it is understood by the war party in England and Ireland.

So, whilst so many of our brothers are out fighting for freedom abroad the master class are, as usual, busy forging fresh fetters with which to bind the survivors when they reach home.

(*The Workers' Republic*, July 3rd, 1915.)

[1] When Sir John Anderson threatened (July, 1940) to suppress the *Daily Worker* he was asked to specify the subject-matter to which he objected. The following reply was received: "The Secretary of State . . . cannot attempt, by reference to particular items, to give you guidance. . . ."

Coercion in England

Two weeks ago[1] we ventured to predict that the power given to the Government under the Munitions Bill would prove to be disastrous to Labour, and we asserted that the British Labour leaders in voting for the Bill, and agreeing to its restrictions, were basely betraying their class interests. Already these statements are fully borne out. The action taken by the Government against the miners of South Wales is the grossest and most unjustifiable attack upon the right of combination any Government has attempted in these islands for generations. Let us quietly sum up the situation:

The miners of the South Wales coalfield have demanded an increased wage, and the revision of agreements made in time of peace, which latter they hold are entirely inapplicable now. The President of the South Wales Miners' Federation, interviewed in London on Tuesday, said that the men's representatives had analysed the figures supplied by the employers to the Government, and proved that the increased cost of producing coal since the war began had not exceeded 5d. per ton. But on the other hand the mine-owners had made this small increase a pretext for an increase of prices of an additional 7s. per ton on large coal and 5s. per ton on small coal, and out of this great increase of prices the miners had received no increase in wages.

Now when the miners threaten a stoppage to enforce their claims the Government declare a strike illegal, and proclaim the whole South Wales Mining area.

[1] See previous article, "The Right to Strike."

Surely a more flagrant case of partiality and class bias was never before exhibited. It means that the employing class have been systematically using the pretext of the war in order to increase their profits; that while the working class was sending their best blood and flesh to the trenches the employers were quietly robbing the helpless ones left behind; it means that this most awful of all wars has been used by a heartless gang of bloodsuckers to enable them to plunder with impunity, and that whilst they rioted in the plunder of the poor, the Government looked smilingly on, but as soon as the poor commenced to call a halt to the plunder, the same Government ordered out its soldiers, and denounced as "treason" the attempts of the workers to protect their interests.

Good luck to the Welsh miners! Good luck to all who attempt to stem the tide of tyranny and robbery which, under cover of military safety, is allowed to run unchecked throughout the length and breadth of the land. Such revolts will serve to unmask the real enemy, serve to show how they who are loudest in denouncing militarism are the quickest to use it to keep their poorer fellow-citizens in the chains the master class are forging for the nation!

(*The Workers' Republic*, July 17th, 1915.)

Strikes and Revolution

We wish this week to congratulate our Welsh Comrades upon the successful outcome of their resistance to the attempt of the Government to dragoon them into submission. We congratulate them all the more heartily because we realize that had the Government succeeded in terrorizing them we might all have bidden a long farewell to our industrial liberties. Successful in Wales, the capitalist class that runs these islands would have been ruthless in Ireland. We are aware, of course, that the people of this country do not possess the same public rights as are freely exercised in Great Britain. But we also know that the measure of liberty enjoyed in Great Britain has a direct bearing upon the measure of liberty permitted in Ireland.

That which the people of England enjoy as a right we in Ireland are sometimes permitted to exercise as a great favour, but if the people of England can only enjoy it as a favour then we will never be allowed it at all. Every loss of freedom in England entails a still greater loss in Ireland; every victory for popular liberty in England means a slight loosening of our shackles in Ireland. This is humiliating, as everything in Ireland is humiliating to-day. But we do not destroy the humiliation by refusing to recognize it. The humiliation is part and parcel of the price we pay for the degradation of being members of a subject nation—fit only to fight the battles of their conquerors.

The Welsh miners have attested the value of solidarity. They demonstrated that the Government feared to prosecute any resolute body which defied them, and to the cautious whispers of those who declared that the Government desired to make an example of them, they fearlessly answered that they were ready any time that the Government wanted to try that sort of thing.

This was the right spirit. It proves again that the only rebellious spirit left in the modern world is in the possession of those who have been accustomed to drop tools at a moment's notice in defence of a victimized or unjustly punished comrade. The man who is prepared to lose his job in defence of a comrade is prepared to lose his life in the same or a greater cause, and out of such willingness to sacrifice the perfect fighting army of revolution may at any moment be fashioned.

(*The Workers' Republic*, July 24th, 1915.)

ECONOMIC CONSCRIPTION (I)

OF late we have been getting accustomed to this new phrase, "economic conscription," or the policy of forcing men into the army by depriving them of the means of earning a livelihood.

In Canada it is called hunger-scription.

In essence it consists of a recognition of the fact that the working class fight the battles of the rich, that the rich control the jobs or means of existence of the working class, and that therefore if the rich desire to dismiss men eligible for military service they can compel those men to enlist—or starve.

Looking still deeper into the question, it is a recognition of the truth that the control of the means of life by private individuals is the root of all tyranny, national, political, militaristic, and that therefore they who control the jobs control the world. Fighting at the front to-day there are many thousands whose whole soul revolts against what they are doing, but who must nevertheless continue fighting and murdering because they were deprived of a living at home, and compelled to enlist that those dear to them might not starve.

Thus under the forms of political freedom the souls of men are subjected to the cruellest tyranny in the world—recruiting has become a great hunting party with the souls and bodies of men as the game to be hunted and trapped.

Every day sees upon the platform the political representatives of the Irish people, busily engaged in destroying the souls, that they might be successful in hunting and capturing the bodies of Irishmen for sale to the English armies.

And every day we feel all around us in the workshop, in the yard, at the docks, in the stables, wherever men are employed, the same economic pressure, the same unyielding, relentless force driving, driving, driving men out from home and home life to fight abroad that the exploiters may rule and rob at home.

The downward path to hell is easy once you take the first step.

The first step in the economic conscription of Irishmen was taken when the employers of Dublin locked their workpeople out in 1913 for daring to belong to the Irish Transport Workers' Union. Does that statement astonish you? Well, consider it.

In 1913 the employers of Dublin used the weapon of starvation to try and compel men and women to act against their conscience. In 1915 the employers of Dublin and Ireland in general are employing the weapon of starvation in order to compel men to act against their conscience. The same weapon, the same power, derived from the same source.

At the first anti-conscription meeting in the City Hall of Dublin we heard an employer declaim loudly against the iniquity of compelling men to act against their conscience. And yet in 1913 this same employer had been an active spirit in encouraging his fellow-employers to starve a whole countryside in order to compel men and women to act against their consciences.

The great lock-out of 1913-14 was an apprenticeship

in brutality—a hardening of the heart of the Irish employing class—whose full effects we are only reaping to-day in the persistent use of the weapon of hunger to compel men to fight for a power they hate, and to abandon a land that they love.

If here and there we find an occasional employer who fought us in 1913 agreeing with our national policy in 1915, it is not because he has become converted, or is ashamed of the unjust use of his powers, but simply that he does not see in economic conscription the profit he fancied he saw in denying to his labourers the right to organize in their own way in 1913.

Do we find fault with the employer for following his own interests? We do not. But neither are we under any illusion as to his motives.

In the same manner we take our stand with our own class, nakedly upon our class interests, but believing that these interests are the highest interests of the race.

We cannot conceive of a free Ireland with a subject working class; we cannot conceive of a subject Ireland with a free working class.

But we can conceive of a free Ireland with a working class guaranteed the power of freely and peacefully working out its own salvation.

We do not believe that the existence of the British Empire is compatible with either the freedom or the security of the Irish working class. That freedom and that security can only come as a result of complete absence of foreign domination.

Freedom to control *all* its own resources is as essential to a community as to an individual. No individual can develop all his powers if he is even partially under the control of another, even if that other sincerely wishes him well. The powers of the individual can only be developed properly when he has to bear the responsibility of all his own actions, to suffer for his mistakes and to profit by his achievements.

Man, as man, only arrived at the point at which he is to-day as a result of thousands of years of strivings with Nature. In his stumblings forward along the ages he was punished for every mistake. Nature whipped him with cold, with heat, with hunger, with disease, and each whipping helped him to know what to avoid and what to preserve.

The first great forward step of man was made when he understood the relation between cause and effect—understood that a given action produced and must produce a given result; that no action could possibly be without an effect; that the problem of his life was to find out the causes which produced the effects injurious to him, and having found them out to overcome or make provision against them.

Just as the whippings of Nature produced the improvements in the life habits of man, so the whippings naturally following upon social or political errors are the only proper safeguards for the development of nationhood.

No nation is worthy of independence until it is independent. No nation is fit to be free until it is free. No man can swim until he has entered the water and failed and been half drowned several times in the attempt to swim.

A free Ireland would make dozens of mistakes, and every mistake would cost it dear, and strengthen it for future efforts. But every time, by virtue of its own strength, it remedied a mistake it would take a long step forward towards security. For security can only come to a nation by a knowledge of some power within itself, some difficulty overcome by a strength which no robber can take away.

What is it of which no robber can deprive us? The answer is, Experience. Experience in freedom would strengthen us in power to attain security. Security would guide us in our progress towards greater freedom.

Ireland is not the Empire, the Empire is not Ireland. Anything in Ireland which depends upon the Empire depends upon that which the fortunes of war *may* destroy at any moment, depends upon that which the progress of enlightenment *must* destroy in the near future. The people of India, of Egypt, cannot be for ever enslaved.

Anything in Ireland which depends upon the internal resources of Ireland has a basis and foundation which no disaster to the British Empire can destroy, which disasters to the British Empire may conceivably cause to flourish.

The security of the working class of Ireland, then, has the same roots as the security of the people of Ireland as a whole. The roots are in Ireland, and can only grow and function properly in an atmosphere of national freedom.

And the security of the people of Ireland has the same roots as the security of the Irish working class. In the closely linked modern world no nation can be free which can nationally connive at the enslavement of any section of that nation. Had the misguided people of Ireland not stood so callously by whilst the forces of economic conscription were endeavouring to destroy the Transport Union in 1913, the Irish Trade Unionists would now be in a better position to fight the economic conscription against Irish Nationalists in 1915.

The sympathetic strike with its slogan, "An Injury to One is the Concern of All," was then the universal object of hatred. It is now recognized that only the sympathetic strike could be powerful enough to save the victims of economic conscription from being forced into the Army.

Out of that experience is growing that feeling of identity of interests between the forces of real Nationalism and of Labour which we have long worked and hoped for in Ireland. Labour recognizes daily more clearly that its real well-being is linked and bound up with the hope of growth of Irish resources within Ireland, and Nationalists recognize that the real progress of a nation towards freedom must be measured by the progress of its most subject class.

We want and must have economic conscription in Ireland for Ireland. Not the conscription of men by hunger to compel them to fight for the power that denies them the right to govern their own country, but the conscription by an Irish nation of all the resources of the nation—its land, its railways, its canals, its workshops, its docks, its mines, its rivers, its mountains, its rivers and streams, its factories and machinery, its horses, its cattle, *and* its men and women, all co-operating together under one common direction that Ireland might live and bear upon her fruitful bosom the greatest number of the freest people she has ever known.

(*The Workers' Republic*, *Dec.* 18*th*, 1915.)

WHAT IS A FREE NATION?

WE are moved to ask this question because of the extraordinary confusion of thought upon the subject which prevails in this country, due principally to the pernicious and misleading newspaper garbage upon which the Irish public has been fed for the past twenty-five years.

Our Irish daily newspapers have done all that human agencies could do to confuse the public mind upon the question of what the essentials of a free nation are, what a free nation must be, and what a nation cannot submit to lose without losing its title to be free.

It is because of this extraordinary newspaper-created ignorance that we find so many people enlisting in the British Army under the belief that Ireland has at long last attained to the status of a free nation, and that therefore the relations between Ireland and England have at last been placed upon the satisfactory basis of freedom. Ireland and England, they have been told, are now sister nations, joined in the bond of Empire, but each enjoying equal liberties—the equal liberties of nations equally free.

How many recruits this idea sent into the British Army in the first flush of the war it would be difficult to estimate, but they were assuredly numbered by the thousand.

The Parliamentary Party, which at every stage of the Home Rule game had been outwitted and bull-dozed by Carson and the Unionists, which had surrendered every point and yielded every advantage to the skilful campaign of the aristocratic Orange military clique in times of peace, behaved in equally as cowardly and treacherous a manner in the crisis of war.

There are few men in whom the blast of the bugles of war do not arouse the fighting instinct, do not excite some chivalrous impulses, if only for a moment. But the Irish Parliamentary Party must be reckoned amongst that few. In them the bugles of war only awakened the impulse to sell the bodies of their countrymen as cannon-fodder in exchange for the gracious smiles of the rulers of England. In them the call of war sounded only as a call to emulate in prostitution. They heard the call of war—and set out to prove that the Nationalists of Ireland were more slavish than the Orangemen of Ireland, would more readily kill and be killed at the bidding of an Empire that despised them both.

The Orangemen had at least the satisfaction that they were called upon to fight abroad in order to save an Empire they had been prepared to fight to retain unaltered at home, but the Nationalists were called upon to fight abroad to save an Empire whose rulers in their most generous moments had refused to grant their country the essentials of freedom in nationhood.

Fighting abroad the Orangeman knows that he fights to preserve the power of the aristocratic rulers whom he followed at home; fighting abroad the Nationalist soldier is fighting to maintain unimpaired the power of those who conspired to shoot him down at home when he asked for a small instalment of freedom.

The Orangeman says: "We will fight for the Empire abroad if its rulers will promise not to force us to submit to Home Rule."

And the rulers say heartily: "It is unthinkable that we should coerce Ulster for any such purpose."

The Parliamentary Party and its Press said: "We will prove ourselves fit to be in the British Empire by fighting for it, in the hopes that after the war is over we will get Home Rule."

And the rulers of the British Empire say: "Well, you know what we have promised Carson, but send out the Irish rabble to fight for us, and we will—ahem!—consider your application after the war."

Whereat all the parliamentary leaders and their Press call the world to witness that they have won a wonderful victory!

Fintan Lalor spoke and conceived of Ireland as "a discrowned queen, taking back her own with an armed hand." Our Parliamentarians treat Ireland, their country, as an old prostitute selling her soul for the promise of favours *to come*, and in the spirit of that conception of their country they are conducting their political campaign.

That they should be able to do so with even the partial success that for a while attended their apostasy was possible only because so few in Ireland really understood the answer to the question that stands at the head of this week's "Notes."[1]

What is a free nation? A free nation is one which possesses absolute control over all its own internal resources and powers, and which has no restrictions

[1] *I.e.*, the title of this article, which was published in a weekly "feature" entitled "Notes on the Front."

upon its intercourse with all other nations similarly circumstanced except the restrictions placed upon it by nature. Is that the case of Ireland? If the Home Rule Bill were in operation would that be the case of Ireland? To both questions the answer is, No, most emphatically, NO!

A free nation must have complete control over its own harbours, to open them or close them at will, to shut out any commodity, or allow it to enter in, just as it seems best to suit the well-being of its own people, and in obedience to their wishes, and entirely free of the interference of any other nation, and in complete disregard of the wishes of any other nation. Short of that power no nation possesses the first essentials of freedom.

Does Ireland possess such control? No. Will the Home Rule Bill give such control over Irish harbours to Ireland? It will not. Ireland must open its harbours when it suits the interests of another nation, England, and must shut its harbours when it suits the interests of another nation, England, and the Home Rule Bill pledges Ireland to accept this loss of national control for ever.[1]

How would you like to live in a house if the keys of all the doors of that house were in the pockets of a rival of yours who had often robbed you in the past? Would you be satisfied if he told you that he and you were going to be friends for ever more, but insisted upon you signing an agreement to leave him control of all your doors, and custody of all your keys?

That is the condition of Ireland to-day, and will be

[1] Although the Irish naval ports were restored to Ireland in 1938, Mr. Churchill now (January 1941) demands their return to England.

the condition of Ireland under Redmond and Devlin's precious Home Rule Bill.

That is worth dying for in Flanders, the Balkans, Egypt or India, is it not?

A free nation must have full power to nurse industries to health, either by Government encouragement or by Government prohibition of the sale of goods of foreign rivals. It may be foolish to do either, but a nation is not free unless it has that power, as all free nations in the world have to-day.

Ireland has no such power, will have no such power under Home Rule. The nourishing of industries in Ireland hurts capitalists in England, therefore this power is expressly withheld from Ireland.

A free nation must have full power to alter, amend, or abolish or modify the laws under which the property of its citizens is held in obedience to the demand of its own citizens for any such alteration, amendment, abolition, or modification.

Every free nation has that power; Ireland does not have it, and is not allowed it by the Home Rule Bill.

It is recognized to-day that it is upon the wise treatment of economic power and resources, and upon the wise ordering of social activities that the future of nations depends. That nation will be the richest and happiest which has the foresight to most carefully marshal its natural resources to national ends. But Ireland is denied this power, and will be denied it under Home Rule. Ireland's rich natural resources, and the kindly genius of its children, are not to be allowed to combine for the satisfaction of Irish wants, save in so far as their combination can operate on lines approved of by the rulers of England.

Her postal service, her telegraphs, her wireless, her customs and excise, her coinage, her fighting forces, her relations with other nations, her merchant commerce, her property relations, her national activities, her legislative sovereignty—all, all the things that are essential to a nation's freedom are denied to Ireland now, and are denied to her under the provisions of the Home Rule Bill.

And Irish soldiers in the English Army are fighting in Flanders to win for Belgium, we are told, all those things which the British Empire, now as in the past, denies to Ireland.

There is not a Belgian patriot who would not prefer to see his country devastated by war a hundred times rather than accept as a settlement for Belgium what Redmond and Devlin have accepted for Ireland.

Have we Irish been fashioned in meaner clay than the Belgians?

There is not a pacifist in England who would wish to end the war without Belgium being restored to full possession of all those national rights and powers which Ireland does not possess, and which the Home Rule Bill denies to her. But these same pacifists never mention Ireland when discussing or suggesting terms of settlement.

Why should they? Belgium is fighting for her independence, but Irishmen are fighting for the Empire that denies Ireland every right that Belgians think worth fighting for.

And yet Belgium as a nation is, so to speak, but a creation of yesterday—an artificial product of the schemes of statesmen; whereas the frontiers of Ireland, the ineffaceable marks of the separate existence of

Ireland, are as old as Europe itself, the handiwork of the Almighty, not of politicians. And as the marks of Ireland's separate nationality were not made by politicians so they cannot be unmade by them.

As the separate individual is to the family, so the separate nation is to humanity. The perfect family is that which best draws out the inner powers of the individual; the most perfect world is that in which the separate existence of nations is held most sacred.

There can be no perfect Europe in which Ireland is denied even the least of its national rights; there can be no worthy Ireland whose children brook tamely such denial.

If such denial has been accepted by soulless slaves of politicians, then it must be repudiated by Irish men and women whose souls are still their own.

The peaceful progress of the future requires the possession by Ireland of all the national rights now denied to her. Only in such possession can the workers of Ireland see stability and security for the fruits of their toil and organization.

A destiny not of our fashioning has chosen this generation as the one called upon for the supreme act of self-sacrifice—to die if need be that our race might live in freedom.

Are we worthy of the choice? Only by our response to the call can that question be answered.

(*The Workers' Republic*, February 12th, 1916.)

ECONOMIC CONSCRIPTION (II)

THIS is generally taken to mean the act of compelling workmen under stress of hunger to enlist in the British Army.

But it has a meaning quite other than that given to it by the capitalist Jingo press, and it is that other meaning we wish to deal with to-day.

Conscription means the enforced utilizing of all the manhood of a country in order to fight its battles. Economic conscription would mean the enforced use of all the economic powers of a country in order to fight its battles.

If it is right to take the manhood it is doubly right to take the necessary property in order to strengthen the manhood in its warfare. An army, according to Napoleon, travels on its stomach, and that being so all the things that are necessary for the stomach ought to be taken by a national Government for the purpose of strengthening its army.

Free access to the railways is vital to the very existence of a modern army. For that reason the railways ought to be taken possession of by the Government on the same principle and by the same business method as it takes possession of a conscript.

The Government does not pay the mother of a conscript for the long and weary years she has spent in rearing the son of which it takes possession. No, it simply pays him a few pence per day, feeds him, clothes him, and sends him out to be shot. If he is shot she gets nothing for the loss of her son, as she got nothing for all the love and care and anxiety she spent in giving him life and rearing him to manhood.

The same principle, the same business method, ought to apply to the railways. All the railways ought at once to be confiscated and made public property, no compensation being given to the shareholders any more than is to be given to the fathers and mothers of conscripts.

All ships come under the same general law. The Empire cannot live as an Empire without ships; the troops cannot be transported, provisioned and kept supplied with the materials of war without ships, therefore all necessary vessels ought at once to be taken from their owners as sons are to be taken from their mothers, without compensation and without apology.

No matter how much the ships cost. They did not cost their owners as much as the bearing of sons cost the mothers. Take the ships !

Factories also for the production of clothes for the army. The Government should take them, for of course you cannot expect soldiers to fight unless they are properly clothed, and you cannot clothe them without factories to make the clothing. So factories are as important as soldiers. The Government is going to take the soldiers from their homes, therefore let it take the factories from the manufacturers. Let it be conscription all round.

There is a grave danger of a famine in this country, as the food is limited in quantity owing to the export of so much food to feed the armies abroad. At the same time there is an enormous quantity of splendid land lying idle in demesnes and private estates of the nobility and gentry. This land produces no crops, feeds nobody, and serves no useful purpose whatever.

By the same law of necessity upon which the Government stands when it proposes conscription of men it ought also to immediately confiscate all this idle land, and put labourers upon it to grow crops to feed the multitude now in danger of starvation during the coming year.

Will the Government do these things? Will it take the land, will it take the factories, will it take the ships, will it take the railways—as it proposes to take the manhood? It will not. Should it need those things, as it does and will, it will hire them at an exorbitant rate of interest, paying their owners so much for the use of them that those owners will pray for the war to continue —for ever and ever, amen.[1]

But the human bodies, earthly tenements of human souls, it will take as ruthlessly and hold as cheaply as possible. For that is the way of governments. Flesh and blood are ever the cheapest things in their eyes.

While we are establishing the Irish Republic we shall need to reverse that process of valuing things. We must imitate those who have so long been our masters, but with a difference.

We also must conscript. We shall not need to conscript our soldiers—enough have already volunteered to carry out the job, and tens of thousands more but await the word. But we shall need to conscript the material, and, as the propertied classes have so shame-

[1] "With the assistance of the Tory-Labour Government, the railway companies are to loot another £14,000,000 per year from the pockets of the people. From December 1st onwards they will be getting approximately £46,000,000 per year more than they did before the war. . . ." (*Daily Worker*, October 25th, 1940.)

lessly sold themselves to the enemy, the economic conscription of their property will cause few qualms to whosoever shall administer the Irish Government in the first days of freedom.

All the material of distribution—the railways, the canals, and all their equipment—will at once become the national property of the Irish state.

All the land stolen from the Irish people in the past, and not since restored in some manner to the actual tillers of the soil, ought at once to be confiscated and made the property of the Irish state. Taken in hand energetically and cultivated under scientific methods, such land would go far to make this country independent of the ocean-borne commerce of Great Britain.

All factories and workshops owned by people who do not yield allegiance to the Irish Government immediately upon its proclamation should at once be confiscated, and their productive powers applied to the service of the community loyal to Ireland and to the army in its service.

The conscription of the natural powers of the land and the conscription of the mechanical forces having been accomplished, the question of the conscription of the men to defend their new-won property and national rights may follow should it be necessary. But as the Irish state will then be in a position to guarantee economic security and individual freedom to its citizens, there will be no lack of recruits to take up arms to safeguard that national independence which they will see to be necessary for the perpetuation of both.

England calls upon its citizens to surrender their manhood to fight for an empire that cares nothing for their rights as toilers. Ireland should commence by guaranteeing the rights of its workers to life and liberty, and having guaranteed those rights should *then* call upon her manhood to protect them with arms in their hands.

Whoever in future speaks for Ireland, calls Irishmen to arm, should remember that the first duty of Irishmen is to re-conquer their country—to take it back from those whose sole right to its ownership is based upon conquest.

(*The Workers' Republic*, January 15th, 1916.)

WHAT IS OUR PROGRAMME?

WE are often asked the above question. Sometimes the question is not too politely put, sometimes it is put in frantic bewilderment, sometimes it is put in wrathful objurgation, sometimes it is put in tearful entreaty, sometimes it is put by Nationalists who affect to despise the Labour movement, sometimes it is put by Socialists who distrust the Nationalists because of the anti-Labour record of many of their friends, sometimes it is put by our enemies, sometimes by our friends, and always it is pertinent, and worthy of an answer.

The Labour movement is like no other movement. Its strength lies in being like no other movement. It is never so strong as when it stands alone. Other movements dread analysis and shun all attempts to define their objects. The Labour movement delights in analyzing and is perpetually defining and re-defining its principles and objects.

The man or woman who has caught the spirit of the Labour movement brings that spirit of analysis and definition into all public acts, and expects at all times to answer the call to define his or her position. They cannot live on illusions, nor thrive by them; even should their heads be in the clouds they will make no forward step until they are assured that their feet rest upon the solid earth.

In this they are essentially different from the middle or professional classes, and the parties or movements controlled by such classes in Ireland. These always talk of realities, but nourish themselves and their followers upon the unsubstantial meat of phrases; always prate about being intensely practical, but nevertheless spend their whole lives in following visions.

When the average non-Labour patriot in Ireland who boasts of his practicality is brought in contact with the cold world and its problems he shrinks from the contact; should his feet touch the solid earth he affects to despise it as a "mere material basis," and strives to make the people believe that true patriotism needs no foundation to rest upon other than the brain storms of its poets, orators, journalists, and leaders.

Ask such people for a programme and you are branded as a carping critic; refuse to accept their judgment as the last word in human wisdom and you become an enemy to be carefully watched; insist that in the crisis of your country's history your first allegiance is to your country and not to any leader, executive, or committee, and you are forthwith a disturber, a factionist, a wrecker.

What is our programme? We at least, in conformity with the spirit of our movement, will try and tell it.

Our programme in time of peace was to gather into Irish hands in Irish Trade Unions the control of all the forces of production and distribution in Ireland. We never believed that freedom would be realized without fighting for it. From our earliest declaration of policy in Dublin in 1896 the editor of this paper[1] has held to the dictum that our ends should be secured "peacefully if possible, forcibly if necessary." Believing so, we saw what the world outside Ireland is realizing to-day, that the destinies of the world and the fighting strength of

[1] *I.e.*, Connolly himself.

armies are at the mercy of organized Labour as soon as that Labour becomes truly revolutionary. Thus we strove to make Labour in Ireland organized—and revolutionary.

We saw that should it come to a test in Ireland (as we hoped and prayed it might come) between those who stood for the Irish nation and those who stood for the foreign rule, the greatest civil asset in the hand of the Irish nation for use in the struggle would be the control of Irish docks, shipping, railways and production by Unions who gave sole allegiance to Ireland.

We realized that the power of the enemy to hurl his forces upon the forces of Ireland would lie at the mercy of the men who controlled the transport system of Ireland; we saw that the hopes of Ireland as a nation rested upon the due recognition of the identity of interest between that ideal and the rising hopes of Labour.

In Europe to-day we have seen the strongest governments of the world exerting every effort, holding out all possible sorts of inducement to organized labour to use its organization on the side of those governments in time of war. We have spent the best part of our lifetime striving to create in Ireland the working class spirit that would create an Irish organization of Labour willing to do voluntarily for Ireland what those governments of Europe are beseeching their Trade Unions to do for their countries. And we have partly succeeded.

We have succeeded in creating an organization that will willingly do more for Ireland than any Trade Union in the world has attempted to do for its national Government. Had we not been attacked and betrayed by many of our fervent advanced patriots, had they not been so anxious to destroy us, so willing to applaud even the British Government when it attacked us, had they stood by us and pushed our organization all over Ireland, it would now be in our power at a word to crumple up and demoralize every offensive move of the enemy against the champions of Irish freedom.

Had we been able to carry out all our plans, as such an Irish organization of Labour alone could carry them out, we could at a word have created all the conditions necessary to the striking of a successful blow whenever the military arm of Ireland wished to move.

Have we a programme? We are the only people that had a programme—that understood the mechanical conditions of modern war, and the dependence of national power upon industrial control.

What is our programme now? At the grave risk of displeasing alike the perfervid Irish patriot and the British "competent military authority," we shall tell it.

We believe that in times of peace we should work along the lines of peace to strengthen the nation, and we believe that whatever strengthens and elevates the working class strengthens the nation.

But we also believe that in times of war we should act as in war. We despise, entirely despise and loathe, all the mouthings and mouthers about war who infest Ireland in time of peace, just as we despise and loathe all the cantings about caution and restraint to which the same people treat us in times of war.

Mark well, then, our programme. While the war lasts and Ireland still is a subject nation we shall continue to urge her to fight for her freedom.

We shall continue, in season and out of season, to

teach that the "far-flung battle line" of England is weakest at the point nearest its heart; that Ireland is in that position of tactical advantage; that a defeat of England in India, Egypt, the Balkans or Flanders would not be so dangerous to the British Empire as any conflict of armed forces in Ireland; that the time for Ireland's battle is NOW, the place for Ireland's battle is HERE; that a strong man may deal lusty blows with his fists against a host of surrounding foes, and conquer, but will succumb if a child sticks a pin in his heart.

But the moment peace is once admitted by the British Government as being a subject ripe for discussion, *that moment our policy will be for peace* and in direct opposition to all talk or preparation for armed revolution.

We will be no party to leading out Irish patriots to meet the might of an England at peace. The moment peace is in the air we shall strictly confine ourselves and lend all our influence to the work of turning the thought of labour in Ireland to the work of peaceful reconstruction.

That is our programme. You can now compare it with the programme of those who bid you hold your hand now, and thus put it in the power of the enemy to patch up a temporary peace, turn round and smash you at his leisure, and then go to war again with the Irish question settled—in the graves of Irish patriots.

We fear that is what is going to happen. It is to our mind inconceivable that the British public should allow conscription to be applied to England and not to Ireland. Nor do the British Government desire it. But that Government will use the cry of the necessities of war to force conscription upon the people of England, and will then make a temporary peace, and turn round to force Ireland to accept the same terms as have been forced upon England.

The English public will gladly see this done—misfortune likes company. The situation will then shape itself thus: The Irish Volunteers who are pledged to fight conscription will either need to swallow their pledge, and see the young men of Ireland conscripted, or will need to resent conscription, and engage the military force of England at a time when England is at peace.

This is what the diplomacy of England is working for, what the stupidity of some of our leaders who imagine they are Wolfe Tones is making possible. It is our duty, it is the duty of all who wish to save Ireland from such shame or such slaughter, to strengthen the hand of those of the leaders who are for action as against those who are playing into the hands of the enemy.

We are neither rash nor cowardly. We know our opportunity when we see it, and we know when it has gone. We know that at the end of this war England will have an army of at least one million men, or *more than two soldiers for every adult male in Ireland*, and these soldiers veterans of the greatest war in history.

We shall not want to fight those men. We shall devote our attention to organizing their comrades who return to civil life, to organizing them into Trade Unions and Labour Parties to secure them their rights in civil life—unless we emigrate to some country where there are men.

(*The Workers' Republic*, January 22nd, 1916.)

in war to force conscription upon the people of England, and will then make a temporary peace, and turn round to force Ireland to accept the same terms as have been forced upon England.

The English public will gladly see this done—misfortune likes company. The situation will then shape itself thus: The Irish Volunteers who are pledged to fight conscription will either need to swallow their pledges and see the young men of Ireland conscripted, or will need to resent conscription, and engage the military force of England at a time when England is at peace.

This is what the diplomacy of England is working for, what the stupidity of some of our leaders who imagine they are Wolfe Tones is making possible. It is our duty, it is the duty of all who wish to save Ireland from such shame or such slaughter, to strengthen the hand of those of the leaders who are for action as against those who are playing into the hands of the enemy.

We are neither rash nor cowardly. We know our opportunity when we see it, and we know when it has gone. We know that at the end of this war England will have an army of at least one million men, or more than two soldiers for every adult male in Ireland, and these soldiers veterans of the greatest war in history.

We shall not want to fight those men. We shall devote our attention to organising their comrades who return to civil life, to organising them into Trade Unions and Labour Parties to secure them their rights in civil life. Unless we emigrate to some country where there are men.

(*The Workers' Republic*, January 22nd, 1916.)